The Art of the
Deal
in
China

Laurence J. Brahm is a political economist and lawyer who resides in Beijing. He spent two decades negotiating investments in China for major multinational companies. More recently, he has established Red Capital Studio, pioneering multimedia productions. He is the author of over twenty books on China, including *China's Century*, *Red Capital* and *China as No. 1*.

The Art of the Deal in China

A Practical Guide to Business Etiquette and the 36 Martial Strategies Employed by Chinese Businessmen and Officials in China

Laurence J. Brahm

TUTTLE PUBLISHING
Tokyo • Rutland, Vermont • Singapore

Published by Tuttle Publishing, an imprint of Periplus Editions (HK) Ltd.,
with editorial offices at 364 Innovation Drive, North Clarendon, Vermont
05759 U.S.A. and 130 Joo Seng Road #06-01, Singapore 368357.

LCC Card No. 2004272807
ISBN-10: 0-8048-3902-6
ISBN-13: 978-0-8048-3902-0

This book was previously published in hardcover as
When Yes Means No! (or yes or maybe).

Distributed by

North America, Latin America and Europe
Tuttle Publishing
364 Innovation Drive, North Clarendon, VT 05759-9436 U.S.A.
Tel: 1 (802) 773-8930   Fax: 1 (802) 7736993
info@tuttlepublishing.com
www.tuttlepublishing.com

Asia Pacific
Berkeley Books Pte Ltd
130 Joo Seng Road #06-01, Singapore 368357
Tel: (65) 6280-1330   Fax: (65) 6280-6290
inquiries@periplus.com.sg
www.periplus.com

Japan
Tuttle Publishing
Yaekari Building, 3rd Floor, 5-4-12 Osaki, Shinagawa-ku, Tokyo 141-0032
Tel: (81) 03 5437-0171   Fax: (81) 03 5437-0755
tuttle-sales@gol.com

10 09 08 07   5 4 3 2 1

Contents

INTRODUCTION
The Anatomy of a Negotiation in China

PART I
Enter the Dragon:
The Etiquette of What to Do and Not Do
When Meeting PRC Officials

Glossary

Annex

Foreword

Cigarette smoke whirled to the ceiling filling the room like incense in a Taoist temple. Chessboard silence filled that area of the room not already suffused with cigarette smoke. One could hear the sound of a tea leaf unfolding and expanding in one of the porcelain tea cups as piping hot water was poured from an aluminum flask.

The foreign party's financial controller hammered away at a plastic calculator. Their lawyer's Mont Blanc pen scratched across a sheet of paper. Somebody on the Chinese side of the table burped. Someone else snored.

The negotiators had been at it since 8:00 that morning. Nobody had left the room all day. Half-eaten club sandwiches and plates of Hainanese chicken rice lay scattered across the room. One of the foreign negotiators stood up and looked out the window of the top floor of this five-star hotel conference room at the traffic whizzing around one of Beijing's ring roads below. It was already dark. He whispered to his colleagues, "When will this be over? ... Do you think we will be able to sign this year?"

Finally, the foreign lawyer interrupted the silence. "Gentlemen, I think we have finally reached general consensus on this one important issue. Now we can begin discussing the details of how it should be carried out. Then we can begin to reword the language of the contract."

"In Chinese or in English?" asked the spokesman from the other side.

Negotiating in China has been described by many as a long and drawn-out process, one which demands patience—a well-known Confucian virtue; persistence—something which comes with time; and survival instincts—something acquired through persistence.

In this era of China's "Four Modernizations" and "Three Representations," many foreign negotiators are realizing that the "way" to negotiate in China may be best sought from the source—China's ancient military classics.

Sun Tzu's *Art of War*, written some 2,000 years ago, is the classic of classics, the ultimate guru's statement of military strategy, which can be applied to all levels of war, negotiation and life. It formed the basis of much of Mao Zedong's writings on guerrilla warfare in the 1940s, and became the favorite textbook topic of a number of professors writing on business strategy in the 1990s.

The *Thirty-six Strategies* is a collection of thirty-six sayings which capsulize thirty-six stories of strategic prowess in ancient Chinese history. Most of these stories are derived from military ploys applied during the Warring States Period (403–221 BC) or during the Three Kingdoms Period (AD 220–265).

Together, Sun Tzu's *Art of War* and the *Thirty-six Strategies* have become a part of the collective consciousness of most educated Chinese. From childhood, the strategies of Sun Tzu and the *Thirty-six Strategies* are learned in school, taught in literature classes, and are even the subject of popular folk opera. They sometimes form the themes of CCTV television serials.

To negotiate in China without at least a cursory knowledge of Sun Tzu's *Art of War* and the *Thirty-six Strategies* is like walking into a minefield without a map.

This book attempts to apply Sun Tzu's *Art of War* and the *Thirty-six Strategies* to actual negotiating situations in China, both commercial and diplomatic. The book is written for the uninitiated (those who have had little negotiating experience in China) as well as the over-initiated (those who have been negotiating in China for some time and may be suffering from burnout). In either case, the reader should be able to relate to the stories.

The stories are all based on fact. They have been written with the intention of providing not only amusement but also some hope when one is left staring out of the window of a business center conference room in a hotel in China, watching the traffic go by and wondering, "When will they sign?"

The Anatomy of a Negotiation in China

Friendship and Mutual Understanding

"Yes" is always the first word in a negotiation, not the last, in China. Too often when foreign investors and businessmen hear the word "yes" in China, they assume that the deal is done. In fact, it is only the beginning of what may often be a long and protracted negotiation process.

"Sleeping in the same bed and dreaming different dreams" is an ancient Chinese saying which reflects two thousand years of experience with partners who may have their own dreams, but are only willing to share temporary accommodations in order to get what they want, before they leave. This is too often the case with business deals in China. The two parties have completely different aspirations and motivations about what they want out of the deal. Thus, they end up getting into bed together on a joint venture and find out, too late, that they are stuck in a bad marriage.

The process of entering into a joint venture in China is like getting married. The parties will first sign a "letter of intent," which is a non-legally binding document which serves more as an expression of seriousness than any binding agreement, that the two parties wish to form a joint venture. This document can be considered as something of an engagement ring.

The marriage will be solemnized when the parties actually enter into a joint venture contract. Before entering into such a contract—that is, during the stage between signing the letter of intent and signing the contract—the parties will jointly undertake a feasibility study to make sure that the marriage makes real financial sense and that it is not all hype and romance. Deals often simply fall apart at this stage. While Western businessmen often think that the Chinese joint venture marital process is bureaucratic, it is in fact very practical when viewed from this perspective.

When the business license is finally issued by the relevant authorities, the marriage is sealed and the only way out is divorce—or arbitration!

Frontline Negotiations

Negotiations in China can be characterized as taking place on two different levels:

• The public level (or frontline negotiations);
• The private level (or backdoor liaison).

Frontline negotiations are those that take place in the boardroom, or the smoke-filled conference room of a hotel business center. These are the negotiations which take place on a public level. Everyone is present and everyone has something or, very often, too much to say. This is why frontline negotiations can take a long time and evolve into highly protracted negotiations. This is why it is necessary to get smart and use the backdoor liaison approach.

Frontline negotiations are, in MBA jargon, "process-oriented." That means they take a long time. To some extent, this is a good thing, because only by being patient and proceeding carefully can both sides really understand what the other actually means or wants. Putting it all down in the contract is another matter, because it is not always easy to reflect what both sides want in two different languages and get it right the first time. This all takes more time and even more patience. Thus, we can call frontline negotiations a "process-oriented" occupation.

The Chinese are invariably characterized as being tough bargainers. This is because "face" is always an important factor in negotiations. "Face" is a concept which cannot be translated into any Western language, but which is somewhat similar to respect, honor, fairness and equality, as well as recognition of all these things together. A Westerner can only begin to understand the concept of "face" when he has had to confront the issue enough times that the concept sinks in. The idea is to give your Chinese counterpart "face" at the negotiation table without losing it yourself.

The Chinese party will also always talk as if they were safeguarding the interests of their company, enterprise, or nation when negotiating with you, especially when there are many people around the negotiation table. This is clearly an aspect of the public level of negotiating. When one thinks that their counterparts are safeguarding the interests of a State enterprise in the atmosphere of a collapsing State enterprise system in a booming market economy and inflation of over twenty percent, one wonders how much the other party is really fighting for the company's or nation's interest.

Backdoor Liaison

While negotiations in China often appear to be process-oriented, the Chinese party always has a distinct set of objectives in mind. In this regard, negotiations can be purely goal-oriented if one is able to find out what the Chinese party's actual objectives are and address them accordingly. This, however, will never come out in the open in formal negotiations at the public level. One must therefore find someone on the other side of the table whom they can pull out of the room, or meet on a purely personal level, to find out what the other side really wants.

Western businessmen too often worry about formal presentations and stiff shirt and tie personal appearances, and are generally uptight about business in the way expected in the West and taught in MBA courses in such towering citadels of learning as Harvard and Oxford. Such learning does not get one as far along in China as learning how to drink, smoke and sing karaoke songs, which can actually pull the negotiations out of a stalemate situation and bring them onto a personal level, and where the Chinese party may open up and actually reveal what is really on their minds.

More negotiation is done in dance halls and karaoke rooms

in China than at the formal negotiation table. Furthermore, the Chinese like to know on a personal level who they are getting into bed with on a business deal. From a practical, operational point of view, if the relationship is not there, then it does not matter how well the figures balance. In a Chinese context, the parties have to get along before they can work together.

Meanwhile, while the Chinese are chanting about benefit to company and country, it is in moments of relaxed revelry that one will get them to disclose what is really on their mind and what they really want out of the deal, that is, the benefit to them as individuals—and, believe me, there is a benefit some-where—and how that benefit can best be addressed.

Likewise, while the enterprise managers have their immediate goals—which are usually in the form of cash—the government cadres to whom they report have their own agenda, which usually runs something like, "How much investment can I attract into my province or city? How fast and how big can the projects be, or at least seem to be, to the cadres above me?"

Through the right type of "backdoor" liaison, one can, if necessary, on finding out what the cadres want, use this to leverage the enterprise managers with pressure from above. Likewise, you can use the cadres below if they will not budge, and by going continually upward leverage more pressure downward, and so on.

The problem is, when someone goes so far up the political lobbying process that they lose touch with the people whom they still have to live with at the end of the day—mainly their partners and the local government officials—the whole lobbying process can get out of proportion.

Many multinationals believe that all their problems can be

solved by obtaining an audience with Wen Jiabao. This is clearly the wrong approach, as these individuals have so much on their hands that the last thing they will get excited about is every single investment project that is brought to their attention. Furthermore, getting the top officials to approve a project does not necessarily mean that the bureaucrats below will act quickly. The days of Mao Zedong uttering a few words and everyone jumping to attention are more or less over. Nevertheless, good relations at the national level can help. The point is that one needs to establish good relations at all levels in order to get things done effectively in China.

Enter the Dragon: The Etiquette of What to Do and Not Do When Meeting PRC Officials

When Entering the Province, One Should Follow the Customs

The fried scorpions sat delicately on a bed of rice noodles. Their pincers were open. Their eyes looked questioningly at the ceiling.

"Try one," offered the Chinese host.

His Western counterpart, a refined and respected American businessman, grimaced.

"He is the Minister," reminded the businessman's Chinese assistant, who was the company's Beijing office representative. The businessman shakily used his chopsticks to pick one fine fried scorpion up by the tail from the central platter. "You do want the deal, don't you?" his Chinese assistant reminded him. Hearing those words—and with his eyes closed—he shoved the whole fried scorpion down his throat, and let it melt in his mouth.

Proper table etiquette can open or close doors in China. In other words, it is important not to offend your host!

At the same time, Western businessmen often cringe at local etiquette which they find offensive or which they simply do not understand or appreciate. Bear's paw, for instance, is an extremely expensive delicacy in China, and one should eat one's designated share whenever it is served.

Likewise, drinking is also a critical part of the whole negotiation "courtship." What one is drinking is not as important as the amount one drinks, and how it is taken, usually by the cupful!

Ganbei means "bottoms up" in Chinese. A proper *ganbei* toast begins with a short speech of about five minutes discoursing on the friendship between the two parties, governments, or individuals, followed by honorific mention of everybody at the table regardless of how friendly they are toward each other, and finally pouring the contents of the glass down one's throat. This is then followed by showing everyone present the empty glass as evidence of the fact that you drank the contents, thereby consecrating the subject of the speech.

One China hand, in order to get through prolonged banquets on successive days, practiced a number of sleight-of-hand tricks—namely pouring the contents of his glass under the table or over his shoulder when everyone was distracted. Unfortunately, this backfired when, on one occasion, he kept hitting the back of the dress of the wife of one of the senior cadre hosts who was sitting at the table behind him.

If your host tops up your cup with fiery Maotai or your water glass with XO, and proposes a toast screaming ganbei, to the chagrin of all the waiters, it is best for you to down whatever is in the glass. Excessive rounds of ganbei (often mixing first Maotai, then Cognac, then white wine, then beer, and then back to the Maotai) often send even the stoutest Western businessman reeling to the men's room.

One must therefore adopt a flexible attitude when embarking on the social aspects of doing a China deal—especially when dining with the power élites who can make or break—in other words, approve or stop—your deal.

The classic case of diplomatic etiquette occurred shortly

after the warming of Chinese–US relations, when Theodore White (who was a journalist covering the Red Army during the war against the KMT) returned to China to see his old friend, then Premier Zhou Enlai. At the banquet, a roast suckling pig was brought to the table.

"I can't eat this," exclaimed White, "I am Kosher!"

Premier Zhou Enlai, always the courteous diplomat, placed his arm around White, and pointing at the table explained in a gentle voice, "But look twice, Teddy, it is *really* a Peking Duck!"

The Dog Acts Fierce When
the Master is Present

Addressing your counterpart directly in formal discussions is another mark of respect in China and a sign of an educated man. While China may be a classless society under Communism, some observers have noted that it is also one of the most hierarchical societies in the world today. It is also now one of the most capitalistic.

Chinese officials meet foreigners who are their equivalent in stature and rank. If your company's CEO and President wishes to meet a Minister or even Vice Premier, then this may be possible to arrange. But if he is the Deputy CEO or Vice President, then he will have to be resigned to meeting a Deputy Minister.

Many CEOs of foreign multinationals still have the days of Kissinger and Zhou Enlai at the back of their minds when they go to China, when what Mao said went, and that was simply all there was to it. They think that the China market can be opened to them as simply as US–China normalization could be had on the back of a handshake between Mao and Nixon. This kind of thinking is, to say the least, fallacious.

"If we can obtain a meeting between our company's President and Hu Jintao, will we be able to get approval for everything we want and open up the China market?" asked one

US multinational's Hong Kong manager (who had been supervising his company's activities in China for years). This is a highly unlikely scenario. In fact, the most someone like Hu Jintao would say to a foreign multinational's CEO would be (and that is under the best of circumstances), "Please come to China to invest. We welcome you investing in China. As long as you invest in accordance with *all of China's relevant laws and policies*, we will encourage and support your coming to China to invest."

The key catchphrase is, of course, "all of China's relevant laws and policies." You will hear these words when your CEO meets with State leaders. Remember, these words are very important. They mean that you open up the China law books and find out what the policies are. You should then go back to square one and invest in accordance with all the procedures that you are supposed to follow, starting from the ground floor and working your way up. There are no shortcuts available on the back of a photo session with Hu Jintao.

The fashion during the 1990s was for the CEOs of US multinationals to fly to Beijing to meet with Ministers and Vice Presidents to "tell the Chinese to stop playing games and open up their markets." (This, of course, ignores the fact that the IMF has now rated China as having a more free and open trading system than that of the US, and the World Bank has rated China as being the third largest economy in the world behind Japan and the US). In any event, many CEOs, frustrated by a lack of productivity at home, flew to China and had meetings with Chinese officials (many of whom responded that it was not China's responsibility to solve America's unemployment problems).

In short, opening the China market is not that difficult. There are many Hong Kong, Taiwanese, Singaporean and

Korean companies that have been very successful at doing this without sending their CEOs to China for high-powered, horn-locking sessions with China's leaders. The fact of the matter is that the latter are more concerned with national economic reform and massive infrastructure development while containing inflation—not an easy balancing act by anyone's standards—than with the fact that the Chinese are not buying enough US-manufactured cars or cameras.

Obedience is Better Than a Show of Respect

Proper translations in meetings with high-level officials can either help set the tone or create discord. Usually when meeting with an official, the parties will assemble in the main conference or reception room of the Ministry or Bureau concerned. There will be rows of chairs for the two parties to sit on. There will also be two chairs at the end of the room for the head of the foreign delegation and for the highest ranking official from the Chinese party. Behind each of these two individuals will be small seats for the translators.

It is best in meetings such as this for the foreign party to make sure that the Chinese official has been well briefed by his assistants as to the actual purpose of the meeting. Otherwise, such meetings can ramble on without ever getting to the point or going anywhere.

It is often customary when engaging with officials formally, to follow the meeting with a banquet. One particular provincial governor was well-known for his capacity to drink enormous amounts of alcohol at banquets. When arranging the formal meeting, his staff asked the foreign delegation's liaison, "We know you are paying for the banquet, but do you want to organize the venue or should we?"

The foreign delegation's leader, however, was very upset, emphasizing that the delegation had flown all the way to China to meet with the provincial governor to straighten out a problem. "We came to China for a serious meeting. Enough of this drinking and eating. We are serious. I want a formal and serious meeting with the Governor."

Everyone filed into the Provincial Governor's office and sat stoically. The foreign delegation's leader began to go into a long diatribe concerning his company's problems in the province. After fifteen minutes, the Governor, in a sweeping gesture with his hand, interrupted the foreign team's spokesman and exclaimed, "OK! I support your investment in my province. Now we go to the banquet for drinking!"

Careful translation can make or break such meetings with high-ranking officials. Take, for instance, the historical meeting between Nixon and Mao's wife, Jiang Qing. Nixon was accompanied by one of Harvard University's best-educated Chinese translators. When Nixon shook Madame Mao's hand, he exclaimed, "Madame Mao, you are very beautiful." She replied politely, "Nali Nali", to indicate that Nixon was flattering her too much. The Harvard translator, however, provided a literal translation of "where where," leaving Nixon completely flummoxed.

PART II

The Art of Negotiating in China

China Hands

It was not just another "China conference" in a five-star hotel in Hong Kong. It was the China conference, held at a five-star hotel in Shanghai. Everyone who was supposed to be seen in the China trade was there.

The economists were there in their gray flannel jackets. The accountants were there wearing their designer glasses with lenses as thick as the bottom of Coca Cola bottles. The merchant bankers were there with their suspenders and gold pins through their collars. And of course, circling around the rest like sharks moving in for the kill, were the lawyers from all of the top law firms in their black three-piece suits, looking to crack the China market.

The first speaker of the morning was the economist. He proceeded to outline his ideas on the whiteboard and to explain that his theory concerning the growth of the Chinese economy was based on a solid set of assumptions and therefore must be accurate.

The accountant, who came next, was from one of the top accounting firms. He proceeded to explain that when his firm prepares a feasibility study for a China deal, it is carried out with the greatest of detail and that all of the statistics which have been developed for the feasibility study are accurate because they are all based on the economist's theory, which is based on a solid set of assumptions, and therefore must be accurate too.

The accountant was followed by the merchant banker, whose suspenders held up his pants over bulges formed from the consumption of martinis and fine foods served in five-star hotels and first-class sections of airlines. The merchant banker proceeded to explain how his merchant bank was best placed to handle "China deals" because their China team had dozens of merchant bankers who traveled widely and stayed in a variety of five-star hotels in China, and therefore they all knew China very well. By the way, they did flotation and bond issues and they would even tie your shoes for you if you gave them enough money. After this dialogue, the merchant banker explained that the secret of their success was that in every "China deal," they would, for a vast sum of money, form a special strategic entry model which would be based on a series of hypotheses which were always accurate because these hypotheses were based on very accurate statistics formed by the best of the accountants, and these statistics could not be wrong because they were based on a well-founded theory, which was based on a solid set of assumptions, and therefore, if one paid for their hypotheses, one would never go wrong entering the China market.

Then it was the lawyer's turn to speak. The lawyer glared at the audience in his three-piece black suit and told them that in view of the China entry strategy formed by the merchant bankers on the basis of the hypothesis, which was based on the statistics prepared by the accountants, which were based on the theory prepared by the economists, which was based on a very solid set of assumptions, that it would be absolutely necessary to put all of this into the contract, and that when negotiating with the Chinese party every single detail of all these points would have to be spelled out correctly in the contract, and god forbid if there was any oversight, and every single "i" in the contract would have to be dotted and every single "t" crossed, and there would need to be at least forty drafts to get by at least a dozen assistant lawyers and their entourage of at least two dozen clerks. And, of course, all of this had to be done correctly and charged by the hour.

The last speaker of the day was not an economist, accountant, merchant banker, or lawyer. In fact, the last speaker of the day was not a professional at all. He was simply the foreign manager of a joint venture company in China. He had arrived in China three years earlier to negotiate the joint venture, at which time he spoke no Chinese. However, by the time of the conference, three years later, he had already learned to speak fluent Chinese, having worked on the plant of the company with the local workers every day since the joint venture was established.

The manager looked at the whiteboard with all the assumptions, theories, statistics, hypotheses, and the dotted "i's" and crossed "t's." He looked at the whiteboard with interest and simply said, "Well, when we did our joint venture, it didn't happen like this at all. In fact, it was quite simple. After days of negotiating, the room was filled with cigarette smoke, there were cigarette butts overflowing from every ashtray and saucer. Finally, in the heat of the last afternoon, the translator burped, somebody misinterpreted what she said, the other party put forward the misinterpretation, we all liked it, everybody agreed, and everyone was happy at the prospect of a banquet. We then went to the karaoke bar and drank XO until 2:00 in the morning when the management threw us out. The next morning when we got together, everyone was in such a good mood that we signed everything right away. Later, we had the translators fix up the language so it could all be approved by the government. Within three months, we had our business license and were into production." Silence filled the room.

Sleeping in the Same Bed
but Dreaming Different Dreams

When negotiating in China, the first rule is not to bring your lawyer along. The second is to throw away your MBA textbook. The third is to listen to what the other party has to say.

Too many Western businessmen fill their minds with preconceptions and spend too much time with their lawyers and accountants trying to figure out elaborate entry strategies and complicated business deals to present to the Chinese party. After all the preparation and the internal corporate complications, they meet with the Chinese party only to find out that the Chinese party has a completely different agenda, such as, "We really don't want your technology any more. All we want is cash!"

Much can be learned from the Chinese saying "to sleep in the same bed but dream different dreams." Most of the reasons for breakdowns in joint venture negotiations, or breakups in joint ventures after the deal is sealed, is because the two parties who have decided to get into the same bed have dreams that are fundamentally different.

Each party has its own set of objectives, its own goals. These, however, may be totally at variance. The foreign party may want to invest in what it thinks will be a great real estate project with long-term financial rewards, while the Chinese partner may only be interested in squeezing as much money as possible out of the costs being paid by the foreign party to remove the existing tenants off the land.

The foreign party may be brimming over with enthusiasm over its joint venture with a Chinese State-owned detergent factory (given China's enormous domestic savings and growing urban consumer market), thinking that with their foreign technology the Chinese party will welcome the opportunity to make the old State-owned factory super-efficient. The Chinese party, however, may be more interested in diverting the compensation being paid to lay off useless and redundant workers into setting up other businesses, which they see as being more profitable in the long run.

Likewise, the foreign party may be busy sending its whizz-kid MBA marketing people to do elaborate surveys of the China market so as to impress everyone with fanciful overhead slide presentations in boardroom meetings, while its Chinese partner is more interested in finding practical tricks and under-the-counter methods of getting the joint venture's products shelf space on the competitive Shanghai and Beijing markets (while at the same time trying to find similar ways of keeping the competitor's products off the shelf!).

Consequently, it is critical to understand your partner in China, and to make sure that your partner understands you. Otherwise, you may find that you have been "sleeping in the same bed while dreaming different dreams," and will realize—too late—that you should have been in separate beds all along.

The Art of Saying "Yes"

One of the problems faced by Westerners when dealing with the Chinese is basic communication. For the Western businessmen, "yes" signals that the deal is done, and the contracts can be signed, and if anything goes wrong, you can always sue on the contract. Right? Wrong—at least in China.

In China, "yes" is the first word of negotiations, not the last. For the Chinese, "yes" means let's sit down and talk seriously. The number of Western businessmen who have come back to Hong Kong excitedly exclaiming that they have a "done deal" is unbelievable.

"They (the Chinese) said 'yes,' you know. The mayor of the city was there, too. He kept nodding his head throughout the banquet. Therefore, he must have liked our idea and agreed. The factory manager also said 'no problem,' so that means everyone must be in agreement. Let's get the contracts ready and go back and sign them up before they change their minds."

Good luck!

When the Chinese say "yes" in negotiations, there is a very fine art in understanding to what degree they actually agree to what the foreign party is saying. For instance, when the Chinese respond during negotiations by saying:

- *ming bai*, they mean that they understand what the foreign party has just said;
- *ke yi*, they mean that anything the foreign party is proposing is possible;
- *tong yi*, they mean that they actually agree with the point made by the foreign party;
- *dui*, there is a range of broad literal meanings ranging from "OK," "Yeah," "Sure," "Why not?," "I see," "Ah-so," "Ah-ah."

Anything short of *tong yi* means that there is no deal. Beware the fact that *ming bai*, *ke yi*, *tong yi* and *dui* can all be loosely translated as "yes."

During one negotiation, the foreign party prepared all the documents and the Chinese party went off to their hotel room to read them. After a while, the General Manager of the foreign party telephoned the Chinese party and asked if there were any problems.

The Chinese party's spokesman replied over the phone, "*Mei you wen ti* (no problem)."

"Does that mean you are prepared to sign the documents?" asked the General Manager.

"*Ke yi* (possible)," the Chinese party's spokesman replied.

"Don't give me this *ke yi* stuff," the General Manager reacted. "Are you going to sign them or not?"

"*Ying gai ke yi* (most probably, maybe)," the Chinese party's spokesman responded.

"Don't give me this *ying gai ke yi* stuff either. Are you signing or not? Yes or no?" screamed the foreign General Manager.

"I'm not sure," replied the Chinese party's spokesman. "I'd better go back and ask my superior."

Contractual Protection

The Western legal mindset understands a contract as a document which is legally binding and to which a company has recourse should anything go wrong. In other words, if the other party "breaks" their side of the bargain, you can sue them and drag them through the courts. Right?

Welcome to China. Five million US dollars worth of equipment is bolted down to the factory floor in Szechuan Province. The other five million is in a joint bank account with the Bank of China. The foreign trademarks are all under license to the joint venture and the molds are in also in Szechuan Province. There is a management conflict and the foreign party wants to take recourse on the terms of the contract through the courts. The courts are not an option because this is not in line with Chinese practice, so arbitration is the only way forward. If the foreign party wins, then this means that the lawyers get congratulated and paid. The rest has then to be sorted out. Who is going to go to the factory and get the machines unbolted, on a train, through customs and out of the country? Certainly not the lawyer.

Is this the fault of the Chinese? No, the fault lies with the Western party who insists on adopting a Western legalistic approach to the practical realities of doing business in China.

What works in law school or in the boardroom of the executive offices of the finest blue chip law firm has little relevance to making a factory in rural China work, and even less relevance to making the people on the other side of the negotiation table understand what the foreign party actually wants to do with the factory once the contract is signed and approved.

What is critical to understand in negotiating a contract is that the contract should be viewed as a tool by which both parties can be assured that the other party understands what they understand, and everybody knows what they have to put into the deal to make it work, and what everyone will get out at the end of the day if it does work. This is the essence of a legal contract in China. One does not want to focus one's attention on the legalities of "what will happen if," if one really wants to get the deal. Rather, the contract should be the tool by which one rests assured that everyone understands everyone else so that no disputes will arise at all and the deal can work and everyone will work together to achieve that goal.

The foreigners who jet into China, anxious to sign up documents in the belief that if everything is legal and covered in the contract and they can go to court or arbitration if something does go wrong, are missing the whole point of doing business in China. Those foreigners who spend a lot of time with their Chinese counterparts and understand how they think and what they want, and who can find a way that makes everything happen for everyone, and who communicate these ideas through clear language in a contract, will be solidifying not just the "deal" but a long-term business relationship—which is what business in China is all about.

Developing a Legal System—from Scratch

When one British merchant banker in Hong Kong exclaimed, "There is no law in China, so how can you do business with the people when they have no law?", he demonstrated to everyone in the boardroom both his arrogance and ignorance.

China has developed a legal system, largely geared to foreign investors, from scratch. Starting in 1979, China adopted its "Equity Joint Venture Law" on the back of the open door policy which was marked by Deng Xiaoping's ascendancy to power at the 11th Party Congress in 1978.

Since that time, China has adopted legislation for equity as well as co-operative joint ventures and wholly foreign-owned investment enterprises, and complete legislation governing all aspects of intellectual property, foreign exchange control, and dispute resolution. In the past few years, China has put in place legislation to govern securities markets, and recently has adopted a Corporate Law.

Within a period of little more than twenty years, China has adopted enough legislation so as to have a legal system as complete as just about any other country in the world. Within twenty-odd years, China has undertaken legal reforms which took Europe some five centuries.

The problem with Western businessmen is that they do not

understand how the Chinese legal system works, and how it can benefit them.

Laws passed by the National People's Congress set forth general principles which are implemented through subsequent detailed rules and regulations promulgated by the State Council (the executive branch of the government) or by the particular ministry, commission, or bureau concerned. One should look to the law for the general principles, the rules and regulations for the details of how the principles should be applied, and any circulars or notices for the leftover details which may be still missing or are unclear.

This system makes enormous sense for a developing country with an economy undergoing fundamental transformations. The law sets the parameters, but after an assessment of the situation (to be read as "reaction of the people") the government will fill the gaps by implementing legislation.

What one needs to be aware of is the shifting policies which often underwrite the law. Understanding these policies means understanding how the government thinks. This way, one can understand the under-lying reason for limitations in the law and play this to one's ultimate advantage in structuring a deal which works practically. In Chinese Taoist philosophy, water always flows down the path of least resistance.

Protracted Negotiations

Often foreign parties are frustrated at the nature of negotiations in China, which are often considered to be long and protracted affairs, something akin to guerrilla war. This is because, to some extent the Chinese will adopt every kind of psychological and even physical tactic to wear down the negotiating team on the other side of the table.

In reality, negotiations begin the moment the foreign negotiating team enters China. Controlling the other party's schedule is fundamental to the Chinese negotiating process.

On one visit, the foreign negotiating team may be met by their counterparts at the airport and escorted with red carpet treatment through customs. On another visit, they may be left outside the airport, without car or guide, until "found" by their counterpart.

The foreign team may arrive in China eager to hit the negotiation table only to find that their hosts have planned a full sightseeing tour for their guests to look at all the old temples and pagodas remaining in the city, followed by a full banquet. This leaves the foreign negotiating team both exhausted and overfed, while the lean Chinese team are ready to begin negotiations at 7:00 a.m. the next day.

Moreover, when negotiations drag on without resolution,

the place to move is outside the negotiating room. The Chinese place great importance on harmony in relations. Friendship is paramount. Banquets with many toasts will warm up the atmosphere. The real deal can often be done in the karaoke bar over XO, when everyone feels a little less tense, and issues can be discussed frankly. If one listens closely enough, the Chinese party may, in such circumstances, tell you exactly what the problem is and what needs to be done to clear it up so that everyone can move on to the next stage of discussions.

As one negotiator commented, "If you do the deal too quickly, they will think something is wrong. So when they want to take you to see the Great Wall, then stop pounding your fist on the table and just go along." Sometimes, the path of least resistance covers the most ground.

Knowing Your Counterpart

The worst mistake that anyone can make in a negotiation is to underestimate the opposition. The Chinese party may not look as slick as their foreign Western counterparts, but they may know a lot more about the West than the Westerners know about China. During the late 1970s, China was coming out of the Cultural Revolution and during the 1980s into a new era of economic growth. In those days, Western imports were new and Westerners found it easy to impress their business counterparts.

The China of the 1990s and 2000s is different. The Chinese have adopted a new kind of sophistication which goes along with being the third largest economy in the world (according to the IMF), and being among the top six nations in the world possessing the highest levels of foreign exchange reserves. Chinese-backed corporations are now unabashedly issuing bonds and listing on all the major markets of the world.

Today, these corporations are adopting a unique management style which can best be described as "market socialism with 'Chinese' characteristics." Once upon a time, a foreign negotiator could impress his counterparts by offering a packet of Marlboro cigarettes and exclaiming "American cigarettes are number one." The last time this author saw a fast-talking

American try to pull this move, the Chinese factory director responded by graciously accepting the packet. He then paused, snapped his fingers and ordered his secretary, "Mei Ling, bring out the Cohiba cigars and Remy Martin Club for our guest."

As one Chinese friend explained to me, "You see, when foreigners hear about Deng Xiaoping's 'market socialism with Chinese characteristics,' they think it is just another one of the Party's jingles. They simply continue to miss the whole point. You see, market socialism in China has *Chinese* characteristics!"

PART III

The 36 Traditional Martial Strategies

STRATEGY 1
Cross the Sea by Deceiving the Sky

Interpretation: Hide secrets in the most
obvious place so as to avoid detection.

Sometimes the most subtle trick is the most obvious. You don't
want to question what seems obvious.

This strategy is rooted in China's Warring States Period.
Some 2,000 years ago, China was divided into various kingdoms which were at war with each other. One kingdom was
named Qin, another Chu.

A brilliant strategist named Baili Xi lived in the State of
Chu. The king of Qin, learning of his expertise, wanted Baili Xi
to become his advisor. The question was how to get him out of
Chu without the king of Chu realizing that Qin was gaining an
advantage.

The trick employed was to accuse Baili Xi of being a fugitive from Qin. As the king of Chu did not want fugitives from
Qin running around his kingdom, he agreed that Qin soldiers
could come and get their so-called fugitive. It was not worth
spilling blood over him. Qin soldiers then entered Chu,

shackled Baili Xi and ignominiously dragged him through the kingdom and across the border into the kingdom of Qin.

The king of Chu, thinking Baili Xi had no value, was relieved to see one less fugitive in his kingdom. When Baili Xi reached the kingdom of Qin, the king received him, clothed him in fine silken robes, and appointed him a top advisor.

When negotiating in China, things may not always be what they seem. The subtle is never obvious. One should never take anything at its face value.

Sometimes Western businessmen coming to China are impressed by what they see. For instance, one Chinese company received the Western delegation at the airport, drove them to a construction site where there were many workers sitting around, and explained that this was where they were building a mega shopping mall and apartment complex.

Then they drove the party to see a field full of ducks and told them that this was their own property, and they were going to build a whole satellite city "like Shatin in Hong Kong." The ducks ran away as the delegation walked over the muddy fields.

Afterwards, they hosted a banquet attended by several city officials who all expressed support for anyone willing to invest in their city. (Everyone ate Peking duck as the main course.)

The foreign delegation went away both impressed and convinced that they had the right Chinese partner with many impressive projects in a city where the officials supported both the Chinese party and the investment projects.

Little did the unwary foreign investors realize that the workers were sitting around the site because financing had stopped and construction could not continue; the duck-filled fields were up for grabs to whoever wanted to put up the cash to develop them; and the city officials would support anyone who came with a checkbook to invest anything in the city. In fact, the local officials saw the Chinese party as only a middle-man facilitating Western investment. (The ducks ran away when investors walked through the fields because they were afraid of being caught and served in Peking style.)

STRATEGY 2
Besiege Wei to Rescue Zhao

Interpretation: Attack an adversary's
weakest point (e.g. attack an adversary's
lieutenant), then divide and rule.

During the Warring States Period, the kingdom of Wei attacked the kingdom of Zhao, surrounding and besieging its main fortress-city. Seeing his predicament, the king of Zhao sent for help from its ally, the kingdom of Qi.

Realizing that Wei's forces were all deployed in full force around the kingdom of Zhao, the king of Qi thought that it would be better not to engage Wei headon (in fact, the king of Qi wanted to preserve his strength and not waste troops helping an ally—but at the same time he wanted to help his ally, otherwise if Zhao fell then Wei would be on his doorstep).

So he devised a stratagem. Qi did the unexpected. Qi sent its troops to besiege the capital of Wei, which had been left relatively undefended because all of Wei's troops were busy besieging Zhao. Wei had no choice but to call off the siege of Zhao and rush back to protect its own capital from the Qi invaders!

When your adversary is busy doing something competitive against you, you can avoid fighting against him directly by attacking his vital parts, which the adversary must do his best to rescue and protect.

This strategy was applied successfully when one large European company was negotiating a major industrial project with a Chinese party from Hubei Province in a hotel in Shenzhen. On the last day of negotiations, the parties were unable to reach agreement on a number of issues. When things really began to heat up, the Chinese party, to everybody's great surprise, suddenly announced that they had arranged lunch at a local Hubei-style restaurant nearby. The focus of the attack had been changed.

The Europeans insisted that they continue with the negotiations, especially as there were critical issues that needed to be thrashed out. The Chinese, however, insisted that lunch had already been arranged (and paid for) and therefore everybody must transfer to the restaurant. Since it was a Hubei restaurant, the European party had no option but to comply.

Lunch soon degenerated into a Maotai *ganbei* contest, with the Chinese party taking turns to toast the foreigners in an effort to get as many of them as possible drunk. In the middle of the banquet, the Chinese also arranged a floor show on the restaurant's makeshift stage (usually used for Chinese weddings). From here, announcements were made that the joint venture would be established, to the great surprise of the Europeans—and in violation of the confidentiality agreement signed earlier between both parties.

Nevertheless, after a ten-course meal and uncountable rounds of Maotai, the foreign party found themselves back at the negotiation table in the afternoon humidity of Shenzhen. Uncomfortable with the lack of air-conditioning and with noise and dust from outside flowing in through the open windows, and suffering the after effects of a starch-enriched and Maotai-soaked lunch, the inebriated Europeans were not in the best position to take a stand on the remaining key issues. The Chinese party, however, had carefully rotated its drinkers so as to reduce and limit the intake of its key negotiators, who remained fresh. "Shall we begin?" they asked. "I think we left off on this issue...."

STRATEGY 3
Kill with a Borrowed Knife

Interpretation: Make use of someone else's
resources to do your job.

During the Warring States Period, Fei Wuji, the Vice Premier
of the kingdom of Chu, was secretly jealous of the fact that the
rising star warrior Xi Wan was favored by none other than
Premier Nang Wa himself. Fei Wuji greatly desired to kill Xi
Wan, but of course could not do this with his own hand.

One day Xi Wan was excited because the Premier Nang Wa
was going to pay him a visit. He expected to have great favors
bestowed upon him. He therefore asked Fei Wuji to advise him
as to what he should do to impress Nang Wa.

Fei Wuji, in turn, suggested that since Xi Wan's sword was
famous throughout the land, he should present it to Nang Wa
on this most solemn of occasions. What a good idea, thought
Xi Wan, who quickly arrayed his soldiers in full gear, and at
strict attention, on both sides of his reception room, and lay his
polished sword before him to await Nang Wa's visit.

Meanwhile, Fe Wuji warned Nang Wa to take precautions
when visiting Xi Wan, as he had heard a rumor that Xi Wan

wanted to assassinate Nang Wa. Nang Wa brushed off the rumor and rode off to visit Xi Wan. When Nang Wa saw Xi Wan's troops in full combat gear waiting on each side of Xi Wan, who was poised with the polished sword drawn before him, Nang Wa decided it was a trap and ordered his troops to attack Xi Wan, who committed suicide in his grief. After that Nang Wa listened only to Fei Wuji, whom he believed had saved his life. As a result, Fei Wuji became extremely powerful.

Mao Zedong's wife, Jiang Qing, used to love screaming "I wish I had a knife in my hand" during periodic tantrums, at which time everyone in the Diaoyutai State Guest House (which she had taken over as her own private quarters during the Cultural Revolution) would go to great extremes to appease her. Using the medium of "culture" during the Cultural Revolution, and the three stooges of Wang Hongwen, Zhang Chunqiao, and Yao Wenyuan (who comprised the other three of the "Gang of Four"), she wielded great power from the Diaoyutai State Guest House using other people to do her dirty work for her.

The strategy of "killing with a borrowed knife" involves using someone else's tool to achieve your own ends. Front companies established in Hong Kong with high-level political backers in China who cannot soil their hands in business, are a perfect example of how this strategy can be successfully applied, especially when they have a Hong Kong tycoon who wants to polish his *guanxi* in China by footing the bill.

One Chinese developed the strategy of "killing with a borrowed knife" into a fine art. Mr Wang, a Hainanese, left China in 1989 (when the going was not so good) only to return to China in 1990 in possession of a foreign passport. Claiming to be a multimillionaire overseas Chinese prepared to invest vast sums in the reconstruction of the motherland, he quickly obtained access to a number of senior leaders in China at a time when China was hungry for investors. Following a number of photo sessions with several Chinese leaders, among them Wan Li, Liu Huaqing, and the late Wang Zhen, Wang took his portfolio of photographs back overseas to demonstrate his vast network of *guanxi* in China. He managed to round up a few overseas Chinese who believed him and proceeded to make funds available as seed capital for infrastructure projects.

With a few properties under his belt and the sprouting of projects everywhere, Wang then dashed back to Hainan, his home base, and demonstrated to the local officials and to his friends there that he was tied up with the power élite of the Central Government and had cash backers as well. A few real estate projects were made available to him. He purchased these plots of land and began to drop seed money on the projects (which involved mostly land speculation on Hainan's budding real estate boom).

Wang then began to court bigger foreign investors, showing his photographs taken with China's power élite and the actual projects which were beginning to rise out of the dust of Haikou City in Hainan. Impressed with this, the foreign investors decided to list Wang's company overseas, and began dispensing money of their own to pay the underwriters, lawyers and merchant bankers. With merchant bankers behind him (all thinking that they were buying into Wang's impressive *guanxi* network), Wang was seen as more impressive than ever in Hainan, with a name card which listed more companies on it than the Hainan Yellow Pages.

STRATEGY 4
Relax and Wait for the Adversary to Tire Himself Out

Interpretation: Exercise patience and wear down the adversary.

During the Warring States Period, when Pang Juan of the kingdom of Wei went to attack the kingdom of Qi, his archival, Sun Ping (the descendant of Master Sun Tzu—who had had both legs cut off by Pang Juan during an earlier encounter) cautioned, "Don't rush into battle against these men. Just wait—take it easy."

Instead of tiring his own troops by rushing to the battlefield to meet Pang Juan halfway, Sun Ping chose to wait in a valley filled with cassia trees. He then arrayed his best archers on each side of the valley's steep walls and told them, "When you see a light in the valley, shoot!"

Sun Ping then wrote a message saying, "Under this tree, Pang Juan dies," and had it tacked onto a tree at the far end of the valley.

Pang Juan's troops meanwhile returned at full speed to rescue the capital of Wei from Qi's siege. Pang Juan ordered his tired troops to push on. In the meantime, Sun Ping's troops relaxed in the valley waiting in ambush for Pang Juan's troops. The troops arrived at the valley only to find it empty and full of cassia trees.

Where were Sun Ping's men? It was dark and nobody could see a thing in the valley. Sun Ping's troops, who were hiding behind the rocks on each side, listened as Pang Juan's men clumsily pushed their way through the cassia trees. When Pang Juan found the note tacked to the tree, he lit a match to read the message. Upon seeing the light, Sun Ping's troops let their arrows fly into the valley.

"An Bing Bu Dang" is one of China's most ancient four-character proverbs. It means "to hold the troops and not move."

Master Sun Tzu counselled in his ancient text, "move only when it is to your advantage."

Wait-and-see tactics are frequently employed in Chinese negotiations with foreign investors who may be just a little too eager to seal the deal.

This is what one American company discovered when one of its representatives was negotiating their first joint venture. They sent one of the managers from their Taiwan office into China on the assumption that because he spoke Mandarin, he would be able to negotiate the deal.

The Taiwanese manager worked diligently to a tight time schedule. He put enormous pressure on himself and his team. But after everything had been done properly and in great detail and within the time-frame, he arrived in China only to find that the Chinese party would not sign. Under the new joint venture scheme being proposed, the contract took all the power away from the old chairman of the factory. The chairman, however, would say little except that they could not sign the contract until clearer terms relating to production were included.

The foreign party went back to the drawing board and worked out a series of production schemes that would fulfill the requirement. Again, exhausting themselves to meet a self-imposed deadline, they arrived at the negotiating table in China only to hear that the contract could not be signed because there was not enough "hard equity" being put in.

The foreign parry scrambled back to the drawing board and after redoing the contract in a rush to meet their own deadline, arrived in China only to hear the old factory chairman suggest that they speak to the local government officials responsible for approving the contract and hear their views. Being a small city, these local officials were, of course, close friends of the chairman. The officials just nodded their heads as they listened to the explanations of the foreign party. They then concluded that some changes needed to be made, but were unclear what form these should take before they would consider approving the agreement.

Against tight schedules to fulfill corporate goal-post measurement requirements, more changes were made which led to cutting a major portion of the contract out, including the controls over the old factory chairman. To everyone's surprise, he signed and it was approved shortly thereafter.

STRATEGY 5
Loot a Burning House

Interpretation: Exploit and capitalize
on an opportunity at the expense of your
adversary's chaotic situation.

During the Three Kingdoms Period, there was a stand-off between Cao Cao and his enemies, Sun Quan and Zhou Yu. Cao Cao lost in battle when the others burned his ships after he was tricked into chaining them together. Cao Cao had no choice but to flee, leaving behind the territory which he had controlled in a state of chaos.

To everyone's surprise, a third rival, Liu Bei, and his master strategist, Zhu Ge Liang, led their troops and invaded the territory with ease (before Sun Quan and Zhou Yu realized what was happening) amidst the chaos, and made the most of the pickings which Cao Cao had left behind.

This was a strategy the British learned from the Chinese after many years of negotiating, and the realization that America's running dog, the United Kingdom, has few real bargaining chips against China, the world's next economic superpower, except America.

For instance, Hong Kong's colonial government generated much publicity by drawing attention to the democratic future of Hong Kong, when in fact history shows that Hong Kong never enjoyed democracy throughout its hundred years of British colonial rule.

What many people believed was that the British Government's real intention was to create a certain degree of chaos in Hong Kong in order to draw international attention away from the fact that the main intention of the British colonialists was to create as many pretexts as possible for draining off Hong Kong's foreign exchange reserves (as was the practice in other British colonies in the past).

Some cynics felt that one of the key tactics being employed to strip Hong Kong of its foreign exchange reserves was Britain's insistence on building a new airport, which resulted in the allocation of lucrative construction and consulting contracts to British companies without much competitive bidding. This airport involved huge land reclamations by filling the sea alongside Lantau Island and also involved the creation of vast tracts of land through the reclamation of most of Hong Kong's harbor, to be sold off to speculative local investors before 1997, as this land was technically under "Crown Lease" until then.

Today, in the run-up to the 2008 Olympics, the Beijing Municipal government has applied the same techniques as British colonists, by selling off huge tracts of land. People are moved off by the brute force of local gangs working for local government so that local real estate developers can use local government permissions to drain the local bank branches of cash to develop huge white elephant "tofu" construction projects, as all involved will get kickbacks from the construction cost overruns. Needless to say, the Chinese are fast learners.

STRATEGY 6
Make a Feint to the East while Attacking in the West

Interpretation: Confuse your adversary's command, and mislead your adversary.

Between the end of the Qin Dynasty and the beginning of the Han, Xiang Yu and Liu Bang fought each other to see who would succeed as emperor. However, in the beginning they were friends.

One day, Liu Bang wanted to leave Xiang Yu's side to go off to another territory, using as an excuse his desire to fetch his parents. Xiang Yu was afraid that Liu Bang might run off and set himself up elsewhere in a rival kingdom. Being clever, Xiang Yu insisted instead that he send his own men to fetch Liu Bang's parents and keep them as hostages, in the meantime letting Liu Bang set off on whatever venture he wanted to pursue.

This strategy is applied to situations where one says (or does) one thing on the one hand to mislead others, while the real intention is to do something completely different.

Mao Zedong applied this strategy over and over again in his battles against the Kuomintang. In fact, at Chi Shui (Red

River), Mao crossed the river no less than four times. Each time, when Chiang Kaishek expected him not to cross, he would cross. Then, when Chiang sent troops to the other side to fight the Red Army, Mao would order his men to cross back. This strategy completely confused Chiang and allowed Mao to gain enough breathing space to move his troops to eventual safety.

Pretending to move in one direction while actually moving in the other is probably the most basic and fundamental negotiation tool which can be applied in either diplomatic or business negotiations (in reality, there is little difference between the two).

For years, China–US trade relations have been dominated by ongoing negotiations over the US trade deficit with China. As China's economic growth reels into an export promotion cycle, the US is faced with entrenched unions, brash industries, and a society which is just too comfortable with the status quo to be competitive against China on the export front. (What the US economy needs is not another invasion of a small Caribbean island or Islamic country to bolster nationalism at home, but a complete revitalization and reorientation of its domestic industry.) The problem is that while this revitalization is being debated in all the committees of Congress, the US wants to keep as many Chinese goods off its domestic markets as it can, and try to force open the Chinese market to US goods.

While this is the fact, obviously US trade negotiators cannot come out and say this directly, otherwise they would not have a leg to stand (or sit) on at the negotiation table. The solution to the negotiation strategy has therefore been to "make a feint to the east while attacking from the west."

While the real issue is the US trade deficit, the issues on the negotiation table are protection of US intellectual property rights in China and human rights. The US does not seem concerned with intellectual property or human rights in other places, such as Taiwan and South Korea (where both are flagrantly abused), but is very concerned with these problems when negotiating with China.

While counterfeit CDs can be purchased in just about any open market in South Korea, Taiwan, Hong Kong, Singapore, Thailand, Malaysia, and India, the US trade negotiators in 1995 demanded that China close down eleven factories allegedly producing counterfeit CDs. This demand was made to the Ministry of Foreign Trade and Economic Cooperation, which is neither the organ in China responsible for protecting intellectual property nor the body responsible for State enterprises.

Obviously, the demands could not be met as presented by the US negotiation team. Therefore, this situation can be used as justification for the US to slap sanctions on Chinese imports. While putting one set of demands on the table and insisting on demands that could not reasonably be met, the US negotiators have created an excuse to achieve their real objective of restricting Chinese imports to help sort out the US trade deficit problem.

STRATEGY 7
Create Something out of Nothing

Interpretation: Turn something that is not substantial into reality.

During the Qin Dynasty, there were two rebels, Chen Sheng and Wu Guang, who wanted to overthrow the Qin Emperor. However, both men faced the problem that they did not have enough supporters between them in order to carry out a successful revolt against the Qin Emperor. In order to increase the number of supporters, they placed letters in the stomachs of fish saying that "Chen Sheng will become the Emperor" and released the fish into a stream.

As the fishermen along both sides of the stream began to catch these fish and cut open their stomachs, they found the messages. A rumor soon spread among the people that Chen Sheng was destined to become the Emperor. As a result, momentum was built to support Chen Sheng in his revolt against the Qin Emperor, and waves of volunteers began to stream into the ranks of his fledgling army.

This strategy involves creating momentum out of nothing in order to bring about something real.

In 1988, when the Central Government decided that Hainan Island (then one of the most underdeveloped regions in China and a part of Guangdong Province) should become an independent province and Special Economic Zone, an unbelievable amount of publicity was focused on building up Hainan to be the future center of commercial opportunity in China. In fact, in those days Hainan was being regarded as the "next Hong Kong" and because of its deserted sandy beaches, as the "Hawaii of China" (two development concepts which are diametrically opposed).

The propaganda which surrounded the development of Hainan Province into a province and Special Economic Zone was so great that even the Chinese themselves believed it. University graduates from all over China flooded into Hainan seeking jobs which did not exist.

There was an elaborate plan to develop Hainan into an area having special technology, manufacturing, tourism, and industrial zones. Between 1988 and 1990, floods of businessmen went to Hainan to find that local nepotism, among other factors, made a straightforward business deal (if there is such a thing in China) difficult, if not impossible.

Nevertheless, the explosion of excitement about Hainan led to an influx of traders and businessmen on the back of hopes that Hainan would be a grand experiment in economic reform. The result of this gold rush was that Hainan became a center of speculation, entertainment, and a number of vices which spell big business, but which are exactly what the Central Government leaders wanted to keep out of China (being the reason why they designated Hainan—an island—to be the target for such experimentation). The result was that Hainan grew and prospered. The graduates landed well-paying jobs.

"Creating something out of nothing" is a tactic regularly

employed by foreign investors as well in trying to get approval for their investments in China. "Technology transfer" rings bells in the minds of officials seeking to achieve policy objectives related to developing an export promotion economy on the back of a program of technology import substitution.

Projects are therefore often approved on the hot air that great technology will be transferred to China and the skill levels of the Chinese people will be raised through the transfer of such technology (which if actually believed would have one thinking that all investors were Peace Corps volunteers in razor sharp suits toting briefcases of goodwill).

"We really care about the people," is a favorite line thrown upon the ears of officials receiving visitor after visitor. Talk of great commitment without cash is one factor which drove the State Council in 1988 to promulgate regulations requiring foreign investors to put up at least fifteen percent of their registered capital within three months of obtaining a business license to invest (or lose the license) so as to prevent big talkers creating nothing out of nothing.

Pretend to Advance down One Path while Taking Another Hidden Path

Interpretation: Distract the enemy by making a deliberate gesture to attack in one direction while attacking another which the enemy does not defend.

This strategy dates back to the Han Dynasty when the legendary strategist Liu Bang wanted to attack his adversary Xiang Yu. In order to implement this attack, Liu Bang ordered some of his troops to cut a wide road in the forest so as to clear a passage for the troops to march forward and carry out a direct attack against Xiang Yu. This, however, was only a ploy to draw the attention of Xiang Yu away from Liu Bang's real intention.

While a group of Liu Bang troops were making noise hacking a path through the forest, Liu Bang sent his real crack troops down another secret path to advance against Xiang Yu's flank without him being aware that the larger troop movement was taking place. When Liu Bang's troops finally attacked Xiang Yu, he was unprepared, having been busy making preparations against the small troop cutting the road through the forest, and was taken by complete surprise.

This strategy involves a sleight of hand, that is, doing one thing openly while really making another, unsuspected, move. Let's see how foreign multinationals can apply this stratagem in opening up the China market.

China knows that foreign investors have been hungry for opportunities to enter the China market of 1.3 billion people. There was a day when foreigners thought that they could sell one shoelace to every Chinese, and fortunes could be made on the basis of the country's population statistics. Consequently, today most international companies have only one thought in mind—selling to China. The question is how best to do that in a market where approvals are still required for many activities and certain imports are highly restricted.

Many multinationals simply want to sell their products to China. But China wants them to manufacture and also to have foreign companies invest in the country so that China can eventually obtain the technology, skills, and productive capabilities of its Western trade partners (and future economic competitors).

Consequently, in order to increase chances for survival in the budding market, Western suppliers have finally begun to realize that market entry can only be attained by establishing joint ventures. Some of these do not even involve the transfer of much technology, but rather the establishment of minimum value-added manufacturing, to allow these companies to get their products into the market. "If you want to be there for the long term, you have to manufacture in the country," said one high-powered executive with an American multinational.

Take one US multinational whose only interest was selling its product in the China market, and cracking the retail sector (a sensitive area at the time this book went to press). It could not establish a retail joint venture, so instead it developed a "manufacturing" venture in a small town, using the minimum investment and technology.

Essentially, the venture was a minor value-added assembly center, used as a base for getting products around the country. While claiming that this was to be its first joint venture to begin product manufacturing through a program of technology transfer, it was, in fact, only a bogus manufacturing operation and little more than a product distribution center.

STRATEGY 9
Watch the Fire Burning from across the River

Interpretation: Allow your adversaries to
fight your enemy while you rest and
observe and later defeat the exhausted survivor.

During the Three Kingdoms Period, Generals Yuan Xiang and
Yuan Xi led armies from each of two of the Three Kingdoms
which were warring among themselves. Cao Cao, who led the
army of the third kingdom, did not, however, lead his troops
against either Yuan Xiang or Yuan Xi. Instead, he held back his
troops and sat on the sidelines waiting for both sides to annihi-
late each other before stepping in.

When in negotiations, watch the situation carefully. If there
is any hint of discord or internal conflict among the opposite
party, then this in itself offers an opportunity. By biding one's
time and waiting, one can allow internal conflicts to bring the
opposite party to a position where one benefits.

The strategy of "watching the fire burning from across the
river" involves patiently waiting for your opponent to have a
split in his own ranks.

China applies this strategy every year during the annual

US–China trade negotiations. The US Commerce Department's negotiators shake their fingers at China and accuse it of intellectual property and human rights violations, when the real issue at stake is the US Government's own trade deficit with China. "If China doesn't do this ... or doesn't do that ...," the Department negotiators scream, "then we will teach China a lesson by slapping tariffs on these goods ... and those goods...."

The Chinese Government then sends out subtle (and sometimes not so subtle) hints to those big US corporations manufacturing and seeking to manufacture in China (who are responsible for footing the campaign dollars which get US presidents elected), that such actions by the US Government may be reciprocated by similar (yet different!!!) action in China. Alarm bells ring.

American Chamber of Commerce representatives from Hong Kong, Shanghai and Beijing send their lobbying teams to Washington insisting that the US negotiators stop their threats. When one former US Secretary of Commerce, Christopher Warren, dropped the tariff threat in Beijing, China's Minister of Foreign Affairs, Qian Jiqian, simply explained that if the US wanted to impose tariffs on Chinese shoes being sold to the US, then China would simply stop selling shoes to the US altogether. Qian made his point by emphasizing that the Secretary of Commerce could explain the situation to America's consumers as well as retailers and the shoe industry as a whole when he returned home.

In such cases, the US negotiators have to cope with divisions on their home front, the US Government, and the US business groups which constitute the ultimate constituency of the US Government. As the internal squabbling heats up, the pressure on China cools down, and the issues get kicked back another year, for another day of negotiation—at least.

STRATEGY 10
Conceal a Dagger in a Smile

Interpretation: Make your adversary
relax and be unaware of your enmity; hide
hostility under friendliness.

During the Tang Dynasty, the Emperor Tang Gao Zhong had a high-ranking minister named Li Yi Fu who was very influential at the Tang court. Li Yi Fu was known for his smiling countenance and for being conciliatory to anyone who was his superior. At the same time, he secretly hated them.

The Emperor did not realize that Li Yi Fu was such a black-hearted individual as Li Yi Fu was always showering praises on him and was full of smiles. The Emperor ignored the warnings of others about Li, believing only in Li's sincerity as gleaned from his smile.

In Cantonese, people like this are referred to as "Smiling Tigers."

Very often one will see this situation in the internal relations of Chinese counterparts. The Chairman or General Manager of a Chinese factory may really carry the respect of his workers, but at the same time will have sycophants fawning over him, lighting his cigarettes, pouring his tea, and heaping praises on him to the point where he himself never knows who his real friends or supporters are.

Others simply enjoy the fawning and believe the words of the sycophants.

This, however, is not only limited to Chinese corporate structure set-ups, but is probably a problem for the readers of this book as well. Just look around the office and see who fawns the most!

The famous Tang Dynasty poet, Bai Juyi, wrote, "The likes of Li Yi Fu are always smiling, and a dagger hides behind the smiles."

STRATEGY 11
Sacrifice the Plum for the Peach

Interpretation: If need be, sacrifice the less
important in order to preserve the vital;
substitute one thing for another.

During the Warring States Period, a high-ranking district leader, Wei Xun Cong, named his son Ji Ze as his successor. He arranged an engagement for his son with Xun Zhen, the daughter of one of the leaders of the State of Chi. But upon seeing the beauty of the girl, the father decided that he wanted her for himself, and banished his son to another region in order to get him out of the way.

The girl later had two sons of her own, one named So and the other named Suo. The father came to love his two youngest children very much and rejected his elder son. The young second wife suggested that Ji Ze, the banned eldest son and designated successor, be killed. However, little did she know that one of her two sons was actually closer to Ji Ze, his half-brother, than to his own full brother. In order to save Ji Ze, the youngest son, So, wore Ji Ze's clothes and, as a result, was assassinated by his mother's henchmen.

The moral of the story is that you have to give away one precious thing in order to get another. The end result, however, is not always what is expected.

Just as in imperial dynastic succession, in equity joint ventures control is the single most important issue for both the Chinese as well as the foreign parties.

The China–Foreign Equity Joint Venture Law, when adopted in 1979, required the Chinese party to always assume the chairmanship of a joint venture. Amend-ments to the law in 1990 relaxed this position, allowing the Chairman to be appointed by either party, subject to agreement between the two.

Under Chinese law, the Chairman of the joint venture is the "legal representative." His signature can bind the joint venture.

For the Chinese party, this position is important as the Chairman of a factory is often an old-time cadre who has spent most of his life with the enterprise and who carries the respect and weight of responsibility of both the enterprise and the community to which that enterprise is attached.

The foreign party, on the other hand, is concerned about legal liability and the dangers of what a legal representative might do after indulging in too many Maotais or XOs in the karaoke bar.

Control is a critical issue for the foreign party as well. Control means the maintenance of standards of the products being produced by the joint venture. Without management control, foreign investors are reluctant to put their cash on the table.

For the Chinese party, control means face and power. For the foreign party, it means quality control and profitability.

The compromise is often an inside deal, with the foreign party giving the chairmanship position away to the Chinese party in exchange for the position of the General Manager of the joint venture. Contracts will be drawn up separating management from the Board of Directors, giving the General Manager extensive control and supervision over the operations of the joint venture, with the Board of Directors limiting its decision making to broad policy and directional issues.

The Chairman of the Board may then have his power limited to only being able to sign on behalf of the joint venture or execute decisions by a vote of the Board, thereby making any independent action by the Chairman invalid.

The General Manager, in turn, will take control of the actual quality and operational issues of the joint venture. In this way, in negotiations one is often able to sacrifice the plum position of visible power in order to preserve vital control on the inside.

STRATEGY 12
Take away a Goat in Passing

Interpretation: Capitalize on your adversary's
negligence or incompetence when the choice is right.

During the early Ming Dynasty, Emperor Zhu Di came to
power by ousting his predecessor, Jian Wen Di, who was said
to have run away and hidden somewhere in the jungles of
Southeast Asia. Emperor Zhu Di commanded that Jian Wen Di
be found and brought back. His famous eunuch-general, Zheng
He, upon learning of this command, took a big navy with him
and sailed off in search of Jian Wen Di.

While Zheng He never found Jian Wen Di, he had a grand
time overseas, using the emperor's navy to conquer other
nations in Southeast Asia. The result was that although he did
not do what he was supposed to do, he was able to get away
with a lot else.

This strategy has since come to apply to situations where
one is able to get away with much more than one expected.

Taking a goat away from the enemy as it passes is easy to do,
especially when the enemy is in a rush.

Negligence characterizes the way a number of Western

companies try to negotiate deals in China. The euphoria of doing a deal in China, and the rush to jump headlong into the market, allows for lots of mistakes to creep in.

As one executive explained, "Don't let your chief executive officer fly in, get bowled over by everyone and everything, and make a promise that will later handcuff your negotiations. The Chinese love it when they know a company's negotiator is under pressure from the boss to close the deal."

When one American multinational was anxious to manufacture its product in Guangzhou, they linked up with a Hong Kong group which claimed to have family contacts in one of the small cities in Guangdong. The foreign party never independently investigated the validity of these contacts. They took the Hong Kong group's claims at face value, and soon found themselves hamstrung, having given away their key negotiating position—the fact that they were very anxious to begin production as soon as possible so as to meet scheduled orders. The Chinese party went ahead and presented them with the contract and related documents, the terms of which were completely unacceptable. The Hong Kong group acting as negotiators had already given away most of their negotiating power by revealing that the foreign party had already committed to a production schedule which was to begin within six weeks of the contracts being signed by the Chinese party.

When the foreign investors complained to the Chinese party and their Hong Kong partners, the simple answer was that "if you don't sign the documents in the form that they are in, it will take longer to approve the project and we know that you are anxious to begin production."

Similarly, the author of this book has lost count of the number of times that foreign businessmen have returned from the negotiating table with signed letters of intent or contracts without fully digesting the meaning of what they have signed. In many instances, they have even entered into agreements drafted in Chinese without understanding what is written in the agreement!

"But we really trust the Chinese party because we have such a good relationship with them. They took us to so many banquets, and refused to let us pay for anything," explained one Western businessmen who brought his letter of intent signed in Chinese to this author.

STRATEGY 13
Beat the Grass to Startle the Snake

Interpretation: Do not tip off your adversary.

During the Warring States Period, the king of Zhongshan had two gorgeous courtesans named Yinji and Jiangji. Each desired to become the king's consort. One of the courtesans, Yinji, had a friend who was a famous strategist and he agreed to help her formulate a plan. The strategist thus advised the king that his neighbor, the king of Zhao, wanted to take Yinji away and have her for himself.

The king of Zhongshan was in a dilemma. Although he wanted to keep Yinji for himself, he did not have enough troops to defeat the kingdom of Zhao in the event of war. The strategist, however, suggested an idea. If the king of Zhongshan elevated Yinji to the status of queen, the king of Zhao could not take her away.

In those days, while it was one thing to covet and even demand another's courtesan, it was considered not appropriate to take someone's consort. Consequently, Yinji became queen, and the king happily believed that by elevating her, he would be able to keep Yinji safe from the king of Zhao.

In the old days, this strategy meant basically flushing out the enemy's position to get what one wanted. Today it has come to mean not tipping off one's adversary.

Sometimes in China this strategy does not work out quite as the strategist planned. An example is the case of a Swedish negotiating team in a major telecommunications joint venture who spent a week in a Beijing hotel negotiating with one of the foremost electronics companies from Nanjing .

On the first day of the negotiations, the Swedish team kept their lawyer out of sight in a back room to provide behind-the-scenes advice as they negotiated with the Chinese party over the terms of the contract.

After the second day of negotiations, the Swedish team debated whether or not to bring their lawyer into the room to negotiate directly with the Chinese party. They thought that as the Chinese party did not have their own lawyer with them, this would put them at a serious disadvantage.

On the third day of the negotiations, the Swedish team, bursting with confidence that the Chinese party was at a disadvantage because they did not have a lawyer, brought their lawyer to the table to add weight to the negotiations. The lawyer negotiated with the Chinese team over the contracts throughout the third and fourth days.

On the fifth day of the negotiations, when the Swedish team arrived in the room with their lawyer, who was by this time exhausted from the previous two days of negotiations, they found a Chinese lawyer sitting next to the General Manager, and the Chinese team primed and ready to hit the negotiation table hard. To the surprise of the Swedish team, the Chinese had brought their own lawyer along from Nanjing for the negotiations. He had been advising them from his hotel room throughout the previous four days.

STRATEGY 14
Raise a Corpse from the Dead

Interpretation: Use something dead to achieve your own ends.

Of the "Eight Spirits" of Chinese mythology, Tie Guai Li was once a handsome man whose spirit decided to leave his body and fly around for seven days to explore the other dimension. Before flying off from his handsome body, the spirit told the others to stand by and wait for him as he would be back in seven days.

The others, however, got tired of waiting and cremated the body. When Tie Guai Li's spirit flew back from the other dimension to this world seven days later, he went crazy because he could not find his old body which was now in ashes. With no other choice available, he had to take the first body which was unoccupied by any soul, and thus flew into the body of a beggar who had just died. Ever since, Tie Guai Li has been depicted as an ugly beggar.

The Chinese government itself has adopted the strategy of "raising a corpse from the dead" in solving its own problem with revitalizing defunct State-owned enterprises.

Today, China is facing a big problem with its State-owned enterprises. During the 1950s, under the influence of Soviet State planning, these enterprises were established not for the purpose of being commercially viable, but to provide people with jobs and a reason for receiving an allocation of income. Efficiency was low and the overall economic results worse.

Through a series of policy measures, State planning has been reduced and these enterprises have had to adjust to the growing market sector of China's economy. This has meant that a lot of these enterprises in a new market economy have no commercial basis to continue operation. With the acceptance of the bankruptcy concept over recent years in China, a number of State-owned factories have become vacant shells.

How does one "raise a corpse from the dead?" China has begun an ambitious program of experimentation with transforming State-owned enterprises into shareholding companies. Many of these shareholding companies are then selected for listing purposes on either of China's own domestic stock exchanges in Shanghai and Shenzhen. Virtually every State-owned enterprise in China is now looking to transform into a shareholding company and find a path to a listing. Some are even selected for listing in Hong Kong and New York City.

Likewise, China's policy of encouraging foreign investment through joint ventures involving the transfer of foreign technology and management skills on the back of capital injections is another means of injecting new life into old corpses. State-owned enterprises, which are notorious for their inefficiency and low standards, benefit from such transfers. Joint ventures are often signed for fixed periods of time, at the end of which the Chinese State-owned enterprise walks away not only with the capital injected, but with the benefits of technical and management training over the course of the investment period.

STRATEGY 15
Lure the Tiger out of the Mountain

Interpretation: Have your adversaries deploy their strongest element away from their defense base.

At the end of the Zhou Dynasty, the king of Zheng wanted to dispose of his younger brother because he knew the latter aspired to become king. The king devised a strategy. He told his brother that he was going to see the Emperor of Zhou. When the king left the capital, the younger brother decided to follow him with troops. The king, however, did not go to see the Emperor, but laid a trap along the way.

The young brother led his own troops out of own fiefdom, leaving the fiefdom unattended. The king, in a smart pincer move, attacked the brother's troops with some of his own troops as they followed along the road, and, at the same time, had more of his troops move into the younger brother's vacated fiefdom.

Chairman Mao liked "luring the tiger out of the mountain." This is probably because he considered himself a tiger in a mountain that others could not lure.

Mao called the Americans "paper tigers." After years of

collapsed Sino–US relations, Mao was to first lure Kissinger, and then Nixon, out of the mountain of America to China. Mao only left China to meet with a head of State once in his lifetime, and that was to the Soviet Union. He never went again.

When Kissinger and Nixon finally made it to China, they never knew when they were to see Mao, until he summoned them. Kissinger and Nixon were resting at the Diaoyutai State Guest House when there was a flurry of excitement outside. Hongqi limousines chugged through the gates, and Kissinger and Nixon were informed that Mao wanted to see them "at once". They were then whisked off to Mao's private villa in Zhongnanhai, where he received them in his own tiger's den— his library.

When negotiating on the adversary's turf, one will always be at a disadvantage. Therefore, it is critical to find a way to "lure the tiger out of his own mountain" to put negotiations on an even playing field.

One German company is well experienced in sending teams to a small city in central Hubei Province to negotiate with a factory. As the factory was one of the biggest local revenue generators, it literally ran the town. When teams went to negotiate, they stayed at the hotel which the factory arranged, and met when the factory managers wanted to meet them. The factory fixed the time of all meals (which were eaten in the factory canteen or in the restaurant owned by the factory). Every night, the negotiators were taken to the karaoke bar and discotheque owned by the factory. Days and then weeks passed without any concrete results.

Finally, the German team began to insist that negotiations be carried out in Beijing. They insisted on booking a conference room at one of the five-star hotels. They even agreed to help the factory managers pay for their rooms—anything to get them out of their home territory and onto neutral ground.

The factory managers finally came to Beijing, where the German company could more easily control the schedule. Negotiations started every day with German punctuality at 8:30, and broke at lunch time. Negotiations then resumed again at 2:00 and ended at 7:00. Progress was made every day as the Germans set goals for each day's discussions—a situation which could never have been achieved if negotiations were conducted on the home territory of the Chinese party.

Let the Adversary off in Order to Snare Him

Interpretation: Do not arouse your
adversary's spirit to fight back.

At the beginning of the Han Dynasty, there was a king from Donghu who was an extremely arrogant man. He demanded that the king of Hun give him his fastest horse. Against the will of his advisors, the king of Hun agreed. The king of Donghu, thinking even more of himself, then demanded that the King of Hun give him his own wife. The king of Hun's advisors were furious and counselled against such conciliation. The king of Hun, however, was especially clever and said, "No problem. If he wants my wife, he can have her," and turned the good lady over.

Thereafter, the king of Donghu looked down upon the king of Hun as useless and weak. As a result, the king of Donghu did not bother to reinforce the defenses along the border with Hun as he felt that the king of Hun was a coward. One day the king of Donghu, feeling proud and conceited, demanded that the king of Hun give him some land along their mutual border. To the surprise of his advisors, the king of Hun said, "That's enough," and led his army across the undefended border to conquer all of the kingdom of Donghu.

"There are some rules not to follow ... and some ground which should not be contested," wrote Sun Tzu some 2,000 years ago. Sun Tzu was an advocate of never backing the enemy into a corner. In his treatise on the *Art of War*, he recommended not fighting an enemy who had a river at its back with no escape. It was better to let them think there was some escape and then attack.

Western businessmen coming to China often hammer the issues too hard, and then complain that entering the China market is like trying to crack the Great Wall. Frustration is common amongst foreign investors trying to negotiate complex contracts in China. The first lesson is not to show your frustration. The second is not to let the other party realize that you are frustrated with them.

It is critical when negotiations reach an impasse to allow the Chinese party a way out. Sometimes this can be done by creating two optional scenarios, putting them forward on the negotiation table, and letting the Chinese party choose one. This will get better results than the foreign party trying to force its position on the Chinese party.

Similarly, it is important to always give the Chinese party "face." Even in a situation where there is an impasse, one should not vent one's frustration. Once harsh words are thrown across the negotiation table, or the Chinese party feels boxed in over an issue, they will become fixated on that issue, and weeks (sometimes months) can be thrown to the wind simply trying to resolve something which could have been avoided by simply giving the Chinese party some options to consider, or several alternative positions to choose from.

Cast a Brick to Attract a Jade

Interpretation: Use a bait (lookalike) to catch something big.

During the Tang Dynasty, the Emperor Tang Taizhong wanted to acquire a famous calligraphic work by the legendary Wang Xizhi which was in the possession of a monk who kept the work carefully guarded. Tang Taizhong used the ploy of having a minister bring another of Wang Xizhi's works to the monk for comparison with the piece held by the monk.

After comparing them, the minister told the monk that the monk's calligraphy was a fake. The monk, disheartened, left the genuine calligraphy lying around unguarded, and went off to attend to something else. The minister seized the opportunity to steal the calligraphy and brought it back to the Emperor.

This is the tactic often employed by Hong Kong tycoons when trying to crack open the China market for themselves. They will make donations and contributions to various causes in China without blinking an eye or—for a period of time— asking for anything in return. Then, when least expected, they will move in and demand certain conditions in return for their investments. The officials who have been on the receiving side for so long have allowed themselves to be brought under an obligation, both real and psychological.

Take Hong Kong's most famous and favorite home-bred tycoon, Li Kai Shing. For years, Li Kai Shing refused to invest in China. Virtually all of his investment activities were in Hong Kong and, later, Canada, but never in China. Nevertheless, the possibility was always at the back of his mind.

His first step was to make donations. He donated schools mostly. A donation here, a donation there, all in the name of goodwill, always sowing seeds of goodwill (and with it an intrinsic obligation) wherever he went. Hungry hands forget today what may be asked of them tomorrow.

His second step was to express goodwill on the political front. When many Hong Kong tycoons were busy venting their anger against China in 1989 following the events of 4 June, not a sound was heard from Li. When the Chinese economy turned full circle and began booming in the 1990s, and those same businessmen who ranted and raved at China in the summer of 1989 began to scuttle back hungry for business opportunities and handouts, Li was already there standing firm in a position of respect and goodwill. He then began to co-ordinate with the Chinese authorities on matters relating to the transfer of Hong Kong to China in 1997. His credentials were impeccable.

In 1994, he decided it was time to cash in his goodwill chips. He asked for a big concession, a huge tract of land in central Beijing fronting the famous Chang An Avenue and Wangfujing, Beijing's 5th Avenue. The Beijing Municipal Government gave it to him—the whole thing—except for the most valuable tract, a corner lot across from the famous Beijing Hotel occupied by American fast food chain, McDonalds.

Li Kai Shing insisted on having things his own way. Having donated so much to China, and having "invested" in so many relationships without asking for anything in return, it was time for him to fetch back jade after having thrown in so many bricks. "If I can't have the corner lot, I won't invest at all in China!" he allegedly told the Beijing Municipal authorities. "McDonald's will just have to go."

And so the authorities told McDonald's that their twenty-year contract would require some minor adjustments, namely, that they would have to move their largest retail operation in the world from its strategically important location. Despite the outrage at this incident among the international commercial community, Li Kai Shing insisted, calling upon all the goodwill which he had demonstrated over the years while asking for nothing, to now ask for and get what most would have thought impossible.

STRATEGY 18
To Catch Bandits, Nab Their Ringleader First

Interpretation: Shoot at the horse first in order to shoot the rider.

During the Three Kingdoms Period, Cao Cao was very cunning and used Emperor Han Xian Di to tell everyone what to do. Every time Cao Cao wanted to do something, he had the Emperor do it for him. When the Emperor issued an edict, nobody dared challenge Cao Cao.

One should never underestimate the importance and extent of interpersonal networking *guanxi* which goes behind the patron–client relationships in China and which makes the decision-making power of certain leaders at times appear to be all powerful.

One should realize, however, that leaders always have their leaders and the chain of command eventually leads somewhere. This creates a situation where the powerful appear to be all powerful, and if one can obtain a decision (regardless of how oblique that decision is) from the top cadre on the totem-pole, then everyone beneath will fall in place—more or less. At least, that's the way the system is supposed to work.

Mao Zedong's leadership role fully illustrates the complexity of patron–client power relations in China. As unquestioned leader of the People's Republic of China after liberation, he obtained an almost untouchable and unreal stature, whereby words uttered from his mouth (taken in one context or another) could be used to give unlimited authority to a certain event (like the Cultural Revolution), when left to those participants in the political in-fighting below to guess what the real meaning of Mao's words were, and to see who would come out on top when the final interpretation would be made.

Deng Xiao Ping held a similar stature in post-liberation China. Although, in the 1990s, Deng resigned from all official posts, given his years in China's military, party, and political bureaucracies, and given the number of interlocking patron–client relations which eventually linked up, connecting to one leader, Deng was in a position to persuade and influence events simply by uttering general principles of direction within which the political strugglers beneath had to work.

Similarly, among some Chinese State-owned enterprises, the chairman or director of the enterprise, if he has his political base and patron–client relations in place long enough, may very well hold strict command over the decisions of that enterprise. In some cases in China, particularly in rural areas where a large enterprise may actually constitute the community as a whole, the chairman of the enterprise may be a "Tu Huang Di" ("din" or local emperor).

Chairman Teng was just such a "dirt emperor," commanding an industrial chemical enterprise of some 1,500 people which constituted the entire city of what in fact was a small town of Hubei Province in central China. What Teng said about the enterprise's operations was law.

When a major European multinational began negotiations

with the chemical factory for a joint venture, it was Teng's lieutenants who met with the European negotiating team for round after round of talks. The negotiations dragged on slowly like a barge clipping down the Yangtze River, without any apparent resolution on any of the key points.

Lack of resolution was further complicated by some internal political jockeying among the several lieutenants who constituted the Chinese party's core negotiating team. Some of the key managers were related to Teng, while others had served longer under him than their comrades. Chairman Teng, meanwhile, sat back at the factory headquarters in an overstuffed leather chair and either commanded the negotiations from behind the scenes, taking in reports from his lieutenant managers, or simply pitting one of his managers against another.

Realizing that endless deadlocks would persist in a situation such as this, the foreign team organized its negotiations in a nearby major city. These were to be attended by the entire management team of the Chinese party and the entire European negotiating team consisting of financial specialists and technical personnel. When all the management personnel from both sides were conveniently locked into negotiations on the top floor of a four-star hotel, the Managing Director of the foreign party, along with the author of this book, got into a car and drove ahead across the province to the factory to meet with Chairman Teng privately for discussions.

One by one, the issues were flashed out on the table, and Teng's basic concerns were put forward. Teng, realizing that he had not been receiving the full picture of the foreign party's concerns from his lieutenant managers, picked up a mobile phone and telephoned his financial manager during the middle of negotiations and uttered commands as to exactly what he should say and do.

The Managing Director of the European party then turned around and drove back across the province, arriving at the four-star hotel the next day in time for lunch and the last round of negotiations during which the main points were finalized as had been pre-decided by Chairman Teng himself the day before.

As the old Chinese saying goes, "when the emperor says 'die,' the people do not dare but to die." Therefore, if you want to get the job done, sometimes it is easier to get the boss to do it for you.

Remove the Fire from under the Cauldron

Interpretation: Wear down your adversary's resources before attacking him; get at the root, take radical measures, and effect a permanent cure.

During the Song Dynasty, Wu Zhu of the Jin kingdom decided to conquer the Song. However, the Song were led by a famous marshal named Yue Fei who appeared invincible. Wu Zhu knew that he could not defeat the Song unless he first got rid of Yue Fei. He did this by arranging for the assassination of Yue Fei through counter-espionage and then attacked.

For Western businessmen, a negotiation in China may seem like a protracted guerrilla war. This is because the Chinese are aware that most Western businessmen are impatient. These businessmen come to China with a fixed time schedule. Hotels and air tickets are booked in advance. Meetings are also arranged in advance—or at least they think they are, until they get off the airplane!

This was what Richard H. Solomon, former Assistant Secretary of State to Henry Kissinger, realized when he stepped off the plane at Beijing's Capital Airport in 1975. He arrived to negotiate a communiqué. Like most State Department officials, he arrived ready to "hit the ground running" and negotiate the kind of communiqué that would be full of all the "right stuff."

The first thing on Solomon's agenda was not a negotiation! "They invited us out to a picnic in the Western Hills," Solomon recalled in later years. "Kissinger was going crazy."

The Chinese kept the entire American delegation hanging on the edge trying to figure out what was next on the agenda. The Americans were champing at the bit waiting for some real negotiating to begin. "The Chinese were dragging things out," described Solomon. Hoping that the Americans would give in rather than miss their self-imposed deadline, the Chinese waited until the last minute. "They then gave him (Kissinger) an unacceptable document at midnight on the last day of the visit."

All too often Western businessmen come to China with big talk and too much anxiety to sign a contract, often without fully realizing what they are plunging into.

When the Chinese party senses that its foreign counterpart is fixed to a deadline, half the battle is won. By simply biding time, the Chinese will often force the foreign side into a position where it is bargaining against itself. An example of such a situation was when one American multinational innocently told the Chinese party that it wanted to be in full production by a certain date. The Chinese party simply dictated the terms from that point on. They gave the American party a standard Chinese contract which had nothing to do with the deal in hand.

When the foreign party questioned the document, the Chinese simply folded their arms and casually explained that it was what the foreign party had to sign if they wanted to start production within their self-imposed time-frame. The Americans panicked and the Chinese had a field day at the negotiation table.

STRATEGY 20
Catch Fish from Troubled Waters

Interpretation: Fish feel lost and disillusioned
in troubled waters, and become easy prey.
Create a chaotic and panicky situation and
the adversary can neither think nor see clearly
enough to respond to the situation.

During the Three Kingdoms Period, Liu Bei took advantage of
the chaotic situation in the city of Jinzhou to take control of
the city. Liu Bei further took advantage of an internal struggle
within the enemy camp to seize another strategic city.

America's giant corporation AT&T has had over a decade of
floundering in troubled waters in China. The company's problems began in the early 1980s when China began shopping for
advanced digital switching technology. While China looked to
the US for technology, the AT&T shrugged off China (now the
biggest market for telephone switching equipment in the
world—and expected to be so for the next thirty years) as
strategically unimportant.

Surprise! While AT&T was unwilling to transfer top-line
technology to China, France's Alcatel, Germany's Siemens, and

Japan's NEC jumped into the market to become China's top three equipment suppliers. It was Alcatel, Siemens, and NEC who caught fish from the "troubled water"—China.

In the mid-1980s, when AT&T finally realized that it could not rely on the US market alone, they plunged into the China market without doing the necessary research and without knowing the telephone habits of the Chinese people. Access to telephones in China at that time was quite limited and the service was generally poor. People often had to queue up to use public telephones, and once they had a telephone in hand, had to wait further to obtain a free line. Moreover, to address the particular characteristics of the Chinese market, switches have to be engineered in a particular way.

AT&T, however, thinking in a typically American fashion, simply shipped its own off-the-shelf units to China. The first switch installed in Wuhan was quickly overwhelmed by overuse and could not meet the demands of the domestic market. Chinese consumers and telephone users complained to the Ministry of Posts and Telecommunications, which in turn complained to AT&T through AT&T's office in Hong Kong. AT&T, in trying to run a China operation, had not even taken tbhe trouble to set up an office in China—another strategic error. The Hong Kong office could not fix the problems, so AT&T had to order parts from the US, along with technicians, and ship all these to China. Over the course of months, AT&T tried to solve the problem, which mushroomed over time into other problems with AT&T's switches elsewhere in China.

Not surprisingly, perhaps, AT&T fell by the wayside as Alcatel and other competitors, which already had established offices with teams on the ground in China, were able to address their domestic problems with speed and efficiency. As one person close to the company explained, "AT&T thought that they could go in and sell switches like it was Iowa."

People familiar with AT&T's operations say that AT&T considered every sale a purely commercial transaction, while the Chinese, on the other hand, looked to try and build, with each sale, foundations for a long-term business relationship. Disgusted with AT&T's attitude, the Chinese eventually stopped buying from them in the late 1980s.

At great expense, AT&T's Vice Chairman Randy Tobbis spent two years in the 1990s shuttling back and forth between New York and Beijing trying to straighten out AT&T's mess. AT&T finally signed tentative agreements with Beijing which included plans for joint ventures to manufacture digital switches in China. It has now finally employed more than 400 people in China and it continues to add more today, in order to address its problems, which continue unabated.

STRATEGY 21
The Cicada Sheds Its Shell

Interpretation: When escaping, do so secretly
without making it public. Develop a false stronghold
to deter the adversary from attacking, then
withdraw secretly, leaving an empty nest.

Lu Bu had served in Yuan Shao's army during the period of the Three Kingdoms. During this time, however, Yuan Shao had never completely trusted Lu Bu. Later, Lu Bu agreed to leave the service of Yuan Shao, but Yuan Shao sent soldiers after him with the aim of murdering him. Knowing Yuan Shao's distrust, Lu Bu created what looked like a sleeping person in his tent and slipped away, thus escaping death.

Sun Tzu advocated, "When strong, feint weakness." Often in China, one does not know who one is speaking with. Sharp American merchant bankers and Hong Kong businessmen dressed in expensive, fashionable attire, will often sneer at their Chinese counterparts, who may appear at meetings in open collars and even jeans.

The China of the 1990s and early 2000s is different from the China of the 1970s and 1980s. While the Chinese may still wear jeans and slippers to meetings, they now carry hand-phones and drive Mercedes. They have adopted a new kind of sophistication. This goes along with being the third largest economy in the world and among the top six nations in the world, and possessing the highest levels of foreign exchange reserves. Having issued bonds and acquired listing on major stock markets in the world, Chinese-backed corporations are now entering the market in a way that was never envisaged a few years ago.

When cigarette smoke permeates the atmosphere and cigarette butts are piled high in the saucers of tea and coffee cups scattered across the boardroom table, and when the Chinese and foreign parties cannot see eye to eye on the key issues of a deal and it becomes clear that the *yin* and *yang* symbiosis of what everyone thought would be a fruitful negoti-ation is about to head into a tail spin, it is time to seek an indirect route to arriving at a solution.

This may simply amount to changing venues, and putting everything on a lighter note. It is often surprising for foreign investors to find negotiations cut off at the pass as they are herded out of the negotiation room and into a restaurant or karaoke bar for further indirect discussions in a spirit more in keeping with "friendly discussions and mutual benefit."

Changing venues and putting things on a lighter footing is a critical game which can be played by both sides. When the foreign party finds that negotiations are going nowhere, ending the discussions and moving to a dinner venue followed by karaoke in a hotel/nightclub would probably go further towards reaching some kind of mutual understanding on the issues than trying to thrash them out over the table. It must be remem-bered also that the Chinese negotiate as a group. This makes it difficult to break through team pressure when trying to put forward an idea. But, by moving the parties to another venue, it provides a much more relaxed atmosphere in which ideas can be put forward to individuals of the other team on a personal level to try to influence their thinking and slowly bring them around to another position when everybody returns to the negotiation table again.

As one experienced negotiator explained, "When you go to the negotiation table in China, the Chinese will tell you that you must make certain concessions because they are a poor, underdeveloped country. Just remember, Japan once pleaded poverty."

STRATEGY 22
Fasten the Door to Catch a Thief

Interpretation: To completely destroy a weak adversary,
leave no loophole for escape; use total
encirclement. If you allow a weak adversary to escape,
he may make a comeback later on.

In 260 BC, the Qin kingdom was at war with the Zhao. Qin general Bai Qi ordered a small force to flush out the Zhao's commander, Zhao Kuo. When Zhao Kuo pursued Qin's forces all the way to Changbi, he walked into a trap of encirclement that Bai Qi had planned. The Zhao soldiers were cut off from their supplies and reinforcements, and were completely annhilated.

Negotiating on the Chinese party's home turf can be a frustrating business. Members of the Chinese party's management may be interrupted at any time to attend to various matters involving the operation of their enterprise, and at any time they may leave the negotiating room to take care of these things—sometimes leaving their foreign counterparts stuck at the table for days waiting for them to resume discussions.

For example, one negotiation team found themselves stuck

in the freezing conference room of a factory one winter trying to make headway with the Chinese party's negotiation team. Negotiations were interrupted by breakfast, lunch and dinner every day. Dinners always turned into massive *ganbei* sessions with fiery local brew. After dinner, the negotiating team would be herded into the factory's karaoke disco for frivolities until midnight. The Chinese negotiation team would split up, one half accompanying the foreign team to dinner and for drinking and disco-karaoke sessions, while the other half slept early in preparation for the next day's negotiations. In this way, the Chinese side was always fresh and the foreign side always looked worn out.

To regain control of the situation, the foreign team invited the Chinese team to a neutral city—Beijing—for negotiations. The foreign side booked the Chinese party's hotel rooms, arranged their meals, and fixed times for working sessions so that the negotiations would be kept on track.

The Chinese were stuck. As long as the foreign side continued to pay their hotel and meal bills, they had no choice but to stay at the negotiation table and finish the deal.

Befriend a Distant State while Attacking a Neighboring State

Interpretation: Adversaries at a distance
can be a temporal ally. Do not attempt to take on
too many enemies at any one time. Another similar
idiom states that a far distant water supply is no
good in saving a nearby fire. The immediate danger
needs to be taken care of first. If there is no short
term, there is no longer term to consider.

During the Warring States Period, an able counsel, Fan Sui, advised the Qin Emperor to conquer neighboring states first while establishing friendship with distant states. The Qin Emperor Zhao Qin heeded Fan Sui's advice and made him prime minister. The Qin kingdom then defeated Han, Zhao, Wei, Chu, Yan, and finally Qi, and for the first time in history unified the whole of China.

Despite 2,000 years of central border friction between China and Vietnam, during the war of resistance against the American forces during the 1960s and 1970s, China was a great support to the Vietnamese government and military. High-level

Vietnamese officials were entertained in Beijing during the 1960s, and Chinese technical experts supported the Vietcong both behind the frontlines and sometimes in the field as well.

During the long war in Indochina against the Americans, from their stronghold positions in Laos, Cambodia, and south Vietnam, the Communist Parties of the three Indochina countries were so close that Ho Chi Minh spoke of their relations as being as close as "lips and teeth."

However, in 1979, the relationship between the three countries changed completely. With Saigon liberated by the Vietcong and renamed Ho Chi Minh City, and Phnom Penh under Khmer Rouge control, the united front of Indochina began to crack. The Vietnamese Communist Party and the Khmer Rouge could not see eye to eye on a number of policies relating to economic reform as well as territorial control.

When Pol Pot introduced his policy of Year Zero, complemented by a policy of genocide of Vietnamese living in Cambodia (later to extend to approximately one million of his own people), relations between Vietnam and Cambodia broke down. At the same time, China, aware of growing tensions between itself and Vietnam, extended a hand to the Khmer Rouge. Pol Pot's first public appearance ever outside the jungles of Cambodia was, in fact, at Beijing Capital Airport where he was met by Hua Guo Feng in 1970.

When the Khmer Rouge attacked the Vietnamese border in the south in 1979, the Vietnamese counter-attacked. Entering Cambodia, the Vietnamese troops discovered one mass grave after another. Realizing the mess which Cambodia had become, they marched on to Phnom Penh, deposing Pol Pot, and across to the Thai border. China responded by attacking Vietnam, to "teach the Vietnamese a lesson," but not without first befriending the distant Khmer Rouge state.

The tragic war of 1979 between China and Vietnam left many dead on both sides, the new alignment between the Chinese and Vietnamese broken, and China extending enormous support to the Khmer Rouge, who continued to fight from their jungle hideouts along the Thai border.

This strained Vietnam's own military resources. Not only was the country stretched on two fronts but much of its economic resources were being channeled into defense. Unable to continue under these circumstances, Vietnam had to eventually retreat from Cambodia. In 1992, Party-to-Party relations were more or less restored between China and Vietnam, and today the two countries enjoy a tremendous border trade.

Borrow a Safe Passage to Conquer the Kingdom of Guo

Interpretation: Help the weak when the weak are not threatening so as to win their support. Mere talk will not save the weak; actions speak louder than words.

During the Spring and Autumn Period, Jin desired to conquer the kingdoms of Guo and Yu. Xun Xi, an advisor of Jin, suggested that the emperor of Yu should be bribed into allowing Jin forces to pass through the state of Yu to attack Guo. Yu greedily and foolishly agreed. Guo was subsequently invaded, but the Jin turned around and destroyed Yu as well.

China has traditionally adopted a diplomatic policy of separating State-to-State from Party-to-Party relations.

For many years China maintained diplomatic relations with the governments of various countries while at the same time supporting the communist parties in those countries, pushing their own policy platforms, which were often different from those of the governments themselves.

This was the case in Indonesia and Malaysia, where China

maintained diplomatic relations with the governments concerned, at the same time supporting the communist party in each place—which had their own agenda against the respective governments.

In other matters, China has championed the Third World and developing nations in providing support for both revolutionary as well as developmental causes in many of these countries.

Shortly after World War II, when fighting broke out in North Korea, China decided to support North Korea even though this caused enormous losses for China. Dedication to helping brother socialist countries in their time of need became a major policy platform of the Chinese. At the same time, China obtained strategic access through such assistance.

Likewise, during the Vietnam War, China sent a number of advisors to North Vietnam and provided great assistance and support in both the liberation of North Vietnam from the French and the liberation of South Vietnam from the Americans. China also provided assistance to the Pathet Lao in their own war of liberation and later even to the Khmer Rouge in Cambodia. While helping the weak in these situations, China also gained strategic access and a greater number of allegiances and influence in the regions bordering China.

STRATEGY 25
Steal the Beams and Pillars and Replace Them with Rotten Timber

Interpretation: Sabotage, incapacitate, or destroy your adversary by removing his key support.

During the reign of Emperor Zheng Zong of the Song Dynasty, the Empress was upset because one of the Emperor's courtesans was pregnant whereas she was not. Feeling that her position as Empress might be threatened if the courtesan gave birth to a boy, she devised a scheme whereby she pretended to be pregnant by stuffing a pillow under her dress. When the courtesan finally delivered a boy, the Empress had one of her trusted servants sneakily steal the boy and replace it with a cat.

The British are masters of applying this strategy to the colonies which they are about to give up. In India, Fiji, Malaysia and Singapore, they drained the financial resources of the country, and changed the composition of the local ethnic population by bringing in foreign labor. This was the colonial inheritance.

In Hong Kong, during the run-up negotiations to 1997, the situation was not much different. One could clearly see an established pattern of colonial departure taking shape.

Having a clear perspective on the colonial history of their neighbors, this is exactly what the Chinese were afraid of—that the British colonialists would replace "the pillars" of the Hong Kong Government with "rotten timber" before returning it to China.

The thing that seemed to be of greatest interest to the British Government in its negotiations with China was the building of an enormous airport. Designated to be located on an island in the middle of the sea, far away from everything else in Hong Kong, and requiring massive infrastructure investment to build all road and rail links to it, it was seen by the Chinese as a way of siphoning off money. The Chinese thought that the need for such an airport was questionable given the fact that international airports already existed in Macao, Shenzhen, Zhuhai, Guangzhou, not to mention the existing facility in Hong Kong.

Nevertheless, the British insisted on pushing the project through. Some suggest that the intention was to use the bulk of Hong Kong's remaining foreign exchange reserves to distribute contracts to British construction companies tendering for the project.

Similarly, the British fought for a "through train" government. This meant that the terms of the pre-handover members of the Legislative Counsel members would span 1997. China's concern was that it would inherit more "rotten timbers" in the woodwork of the Hong Kong Government. To some extent, this is what happened.

STRATEGY 26
Point at the Mulberry but Curse the Locust

Interpretation: Make use of a subject
as a pretext to express one's objections.

During the regime of Emperor Xianzong of the Ming Dynasty,
there was an evil eunuch named Wang Zhi. Wang Zhi was very
close to the Emperor. He had acquired a lot of power which
had made him a very dangerous adversary.

One day, an actor in the imperial court named A Chou gave
a performance before the court in which he portrayed a drunk-
ard. In this role, he was very free with his comments. As part of
the performance, another actor suddenly warned him to stop
his singing and acting because a high-ranking Mandarin was
approaching the performance area. A Chou replied, "I am not
afraid of a high-ranking mandarin," and kept on dancing and
making jokes. Next, he heard a warning that the Emperor
himself would be passing by. He continued making jokes and
indicated that he was not afraid even of the Emperor. Then a
warning came that the eunuch Wang Zhi would be approaching. A Chou suddenly fell to his knees saying, "Death penalty
is my dessert! Death penalty is my dessert! I am not afraid

of the Emperor, but I am afraid of Eunuch Wang Zhi."

By expressing his fear of the eunuch more than of the Emperor, A Chou was indirectly letting everybody know that Wang Zhi was a dangerous man and even the Emperor should be careful. In a subtle way, he criticized the Emperor for his foolishness in failing to distinguish those subordinates faithful to him from those who were evil.

The use of this strategy (to point at the mulberry but curse the locust) means to borrow or use one thing to achieve another.

A good example of this strategy was seen in a US–China trade dispute.

"Point at the mulberry and curse the locust" is an ancient Chinese proverb, but it is one that the United States Government's trade negotiators have learned well. Translated into not-so-oblique language, it might go, "Point at the US trade deficit and curse China's foreign exchange system and China's failure to protect intellectual property rights."

Lacking better tools with which to negotiate reducing America's ballooning trade deficit with China, the US pressed ahead with its negative campaign. Then, Treasury Under Secretary Lawrence Summers accused China of manipulating its foreign exchange system to prevent an effective balance of payments adjustment. He threatened to prevent China's entry into the WTO if the situation were not corrected.

STRATEGY 27
Play Dumb

Interpretation: Let your adversary underestimate your capabilities.

During the Three Kingdoms Period, Sima Yi played dumb so as to let Cao Shuang think that he was weak, ill and useless. Sima Yi, however, used the opportunity to catch Cao Shuang off-guard and kill him, thereby assuming command himself.

The worst mistake anyone can make in a negotiating situation in China is to underestimate the opposition. Western negotiators arriving in China in their sharp business suits and branded suspenders often sneer when they enter the negotiating room to find their counterparts wearing jeans and slippers, and smoking endless rounds of cigarettes.

While the Chinese party may not look as slick as their foreign Western counterparts, they may know a lot more about the West than the Westerners whom they are dealing with know or can even imagine about China.

During the late 1970s, China was coming out of the Cultural Revolution, and by the 1980s it was entering a new era of economic growth. In those days, Western imports were new, and Westerners found it easy to impress their counterparts by simply being Western.

In 1988, a Hong Kong delegation of businessmen visited Shanghai and to their surprise found the Mayor showing up for the meeting in a pair of hiking boots (probably having just come from inspecting some site). The Hong Kong businessmen, with their impressive Rolex watches and other Western acoutrements, sniggered among themselves, whispering in imitation British accents, "Oh, how terrible! Look at the way the Mayor dresses. Simply terrible!" They did not realize that Zhu Rongji, then Mayor, would become Vice Premier only five years later. The "financial czar" of China would go on to institute some of the most progressive financial reforms that the country has ever seen.

While foreign managers bring operational techniques and analytical abilities with them to China, they often hit a brick wall as they enter the China market for not being able to understand the distribution and sales tricks which their Chinese counterparts have so successfully developed in order to overcome inter-provincial protectionism and a market where business relationships are all important in cracking the domestic market.

Even though Western businessmen may be flashing out statistics on fancy calculators, they may be making unrealistic predictions about sales volumes and profits, which are not possible to achieve in the China market without adopting the kind of "backdoor" techniques the Chinese have developed as a matter of survival (such as using State-subsidized raw materials and goods to undercut market prices).

STRATEGY 28
Remove the Ladder after Your Ascent

Interpretation: Lure an adversary into a trap, then cut him off.

This strategy comes from the Three Kingdoms Period, when a young warlord was caught in a family feud and sought the advice of the master strategist Zhu Ge Liang. Although Zhu Ge Liang went to visit the young warlord when summoned, it was with reluctance as he had no desire to get involved in a family dispute.

The warlord cleverly invited Zhu Ge Liang to join him in his library upstairs to view his collection of rare and classic books. Zhu Ge Liang complied, only to find that the ladder had been removed after ascending to the library. He himself had been outwitted. With no way out, he agreed to advise the young warlord.

Mao Zedong adopted the strategy of "luring the enemy in deep, avoiding his main force and striking at his weak spots."

Again and again, Mao Zedong employed this strategy in luring Chiang Kaishek's troops deep into "Red base" areas, and trapping them when they pushed "straight ahead" and in too deep. Mao Zedong described this strategy, citing a scene in the classical novel *Outlaws of the Marsh*. He wrote:

"We all know that when two boxers fight, the clever boxer usually gives a little ground at first, while the foolish one rushes in furiously and uses up his resources at the very start, and in the end he is often beaten by the man who has given ground. In the novel *Outlaws of the Marsh*, the drill master Hang, challenging Lin Chong to fight on Chai Jin's estate, shouts 'Come on! Come on!' In the end, it is the retreating Lin Chong who spots Hang's weak point and floors him with one blow."

That is what happened to one Jardine Matheson Holdings Ltd employee who went to Xianfan in the middle of winter to finalize contract discussions for the purchase of ball bearings. To his surprise, the factory manager raised the price.

His efforts at haggling were to no avail. As the Jardine Matheson employee recalled later, "It was freezing cold, and the guest house at the factory had no hot water and no shower. I wore gloves in the dining room."

When it became clear to the Jardine Matheson employee that the negotiations were leading nowhere, he decided to leave town. At least he thought he could leave town. But he was in for a surprise. The factory officials told the Jardine Matheson employee, "Sorry, we can't help you get a train ticket." Then the employee decided to get transport to the train station to see if he might have better luck buying a ticket direct. "Sorry," explained the factory officials. "Our shuttle bus is busy with other matters." The employee had no choice but to stay put. The shuttle bus remained "busy" for a few more days in the hope that the employee would agree to the new price terms. He didn't. So one day, the Chinese factory sent the shuttle bus to take the frozen Jardine man to the train station to leave.

STRATEGY 29
Decorate the Tree with Fake Blossoms

Interpretation: Exaggerate in order to mislead your adversary, letting him believe that you are very strong.

Emperor Yangdi of the Sui Dynasty built the Grand Canal in order to strengthen China's economy. At the same time, he went out of his way to impress foreign visitors by ordering restaurants not to charge them for meals and to tell them that "China is so rich that people don't need to pay for their meals." In winter, he had the bare trees around the capital at Loyang decorated with silk flowers. Upon leaving Loyang, the travellers could see the harsh reality of the countryside, and would realize that the silk flowers were just for show.

When tourists arrive in China, they are often greeted by swarms of kindergarten children waving little flags and singing songs of welcome. When foreign investors arrive, they are taken on factory visits and shown well-organized production teams and well-orchestrated demonstrations of government support for the factory. This often includes local government leaders singing the praises of the enterprise and acknowledging the preferential treatment available if foreigners invest there.

The Chinese are masters at putting on a show. When heads of State visit China, the streets are well cleaned beforehand and crowds are mobilized to cheer the motorcade. This treatment is guaranteed to leave a deep and lasting impression.

When the Chairman of the Board of a foreign multi-national comes to China, he is often given VIP treatment at Beijing's Capital Airport. He is greeted with a Mercedes Benz, and a police escort takes him to the cavernous Great Hall of the People outfitted with dazzling red carpets and some of the most outlandish and expensive pieces of Chinese art. This, however, is a far cry from the reality of managing State workers on a factory floor, which the CEO's company may be about to invest in. As one foreign company representative commented, "The last thing you want is for your CEO to come to China on a whirlwind trip, get dazzled by the treatment, make promises, and leave you to negotiate the details."

Turn Yourself into a Host from Being a Guest

Interpretation: Exchange your place or position, and reverse the situation.

When Liu Bang and Xiang Yu led a successful rebellion against the Qin Emperor, Liu Bang entered the Imperial Palace first, leaving Xiang Yu (who possessed the bigger force of the two) to carry out mopping-up operations in the provinces. As Liu Bang was about to settle down to his first evening in the palace with the toppled emperor's retinue of concubines, an advisor reminded him that Xiang Yu would be the real "host" when he returned and that Liu Bang was only a "guest," since Xiang Yu had almost four times as many troops as Liu Bang.

Liu Bang, taking his advice, decided to leave the palace. When Xiang Yu returned and settled into the palace, he became besotted with concubines and palace pleasures. Meanwhile, Liu Bang built up his forces, and when strong enough returned to evict Xiang Yu. (Xiang Yu and his favorite courtesan both slit their throats as they were fleeing.)

Turning yourself into a host after being a guest is a classic strategy for reversing positions and salvaging the situation.

Tired of having to drink toasts to officials through banquet after banquet in China, Karl Heinz Ege, a German representative who has been living in China for four years, decided to bring a bottle of German Schnapps to banquets. When the Maotai *ganbei*-ing situation got out of control, Ege would pull the bottle of Schnapps out of a paper bag he kept under the table and begin filling the glasses of his hosts, insisting that they try "German Maotai." The officials winced and grimaced as each one forced the Schnapps down their throats. Faces turned red and then white The toasting ritual subsided into a mild exchange of courtesies.

The most classic example of being turned from a guest into a host occurred when one European company, seeking to obtain the support of the provincial government, decided to go on a lobbying mission to meet the governor of the province. The managing director of the European company, however, insisted to his staff that "This was to be a serious meeting" and "that there is to be no banqueting or drinking with the Chinese officials," and "we must be serious and make them know that we are serious about the issues at hand."

When the managers on the ground were arranging for their boss to arrive for the meetings, the provincial government's foreign affairs office (expecting the foreign party to host the dinner, of course) asked, "For the dinner you are hosting for the governor, do you want to book the restaurant or should we book it for you?" The staff, too embarrassed to explain their boss's view on the subject, simply let the provincial government make the arrangements. When the managing director of the European company arrived to meet with the governor of the province for "serious formal discussions," the meeting lasted a mere fifteen minutes. The governor simply said, "I support your project, now let's go and have dinner and drink."

The European company's managing director then found out that he was hosting dinner for a number of provincial government officials who consumed several bottles of XO and exotic (and expensive) bear's paw at the expense of their foreign company. The foreign party then found to their surprise that the provincial government also hit them with a bill for renting the meeting room for their meeting with the governor.

STRATEGY 31
Use a Beauty to Ensnare a Man

Interpretation: Intoxicate or indulge your
adversary with a time- or energy-absorbing activity,
thereby diminishing his spirit to fight.

During the Eastern Han Dynasty, the Prime Minister, Dong Zhuo, was a debauched tyrant, ruling for the boy emperor. One court official, Wang Yun, thought of a way to defeat Dong Zhuo.

Wang Yun collaborated with his beautiful daughter in the plot. Wang promised his daughter to both Dong Zhuo and Lu Bu, Dong Zhuo's loyal Commander-General of the military. The daughter used her charms on both men. Dong Zhuo, as Prime Minister, ordered Lu Bu to keep his hands off the girl. Lu Bu, as commander of the military, killed Dong Zhuo. Wang's daughter was left smiling.

This is the oldest trick in the book. The Chinese love sending attractive young women as translators to meetings with middle-aged (and older) executives. It makes the executives talk. The translators just need to listen.

This is also an easy strategy for the Chinese party to adopt if they want to get rid of the foreign manager of a joint venture but are too polite to voice their views openly at a board meeting. Foreign managers who are alone in China for too long are prone to weakness. They are an easy pickup, and an easier nab by the police.

When found with a prostitute, the police will stamp the word "prostitute" on every page of a foreigner's passport and ignominiously send him off at the nearest airport. One Australian executive was so proud at having been arrested in China for a "sexual offense" that he had his red-chopped passport framed.

STRATEGY 32
Open the Gate of an Undefended City

Interpretation: Generate doubts in an
adversary's camp by presenting something that
is really simple. Let your adversary overestimate
your capabilities.

During the Three Kingdoms Period, master statesman and
strategist Zhu Ge Liang, upon seeing his city-fortress surrounded by a large number of hostile enemy troops, used this
strategy: he opened wide the gates of the besieged city and
showed the enemy forces the empty streets within. Disarmed at
seeing only dustsweepers brushing the dust away from the open
gate and fearing a trick, the enemy immediately retreated and
gave up their plan to besiege the city.

Tours to model factories and words of "everything is OK" or
"no problem" often do more to scare away investors than attract
them.

Western businessmen often plough through their negotiations without realizing that the Chinese party nodding their
heads on the other side of the table may not have agreed to any
of the conditions or terms which the foreign businessmen are

ticking off as they go through their contract. They assume from the nods that agreement has been obtained from the other side.

As mentioned earlier, in Part II of this book, "yes" in China can be a broad interpretation for a number of responses from the Chinese party. It may, in fact, really mean "Yes, I will think about it" or, even better, "It sounds OK." (Refer to Part II: The Art of Saying "Yes" for a list of possible positive responses given by the Chinese during a negotiation.)

Take, for instance, the foreign party entering into a technology transfer agreement who sat all night at a banquet with the governor of the city and the Chinese party. They were so convinced that the deal was agreed that they returned to Beijing to tell their lawyers to draw up the contracts because "the governor kept nodding his head throughout the dinner. Therefore, he must be supporting our projects." The Chinese factory chairman had mentioned to them afterwards that "everything was OK and that there was no problem." In fact, this just means that "based on the present situation, everything *should* be OK and that there *should* be no problem." But, as time goes on, there may be a lot of (new) problems arising, so the terms and conditions agreed upon earlier should be discussed again (and again) when the time comes. (Please note the "But's" after their "Yes's".)

Use Your Adversary's Spies to Sow Discord in Your Adversary's Camp

Interpretation: Spread wrong information. Sow distrust or dissension among one's enemies through counter-espionage.

During the Three Kingdoms Period, Zhou Yu used Cao Cao's spy to give misinformation to Cao Cao, leading Cao Cao to kill his own able navy commanders. This left Cao Cao without anyone qualified to command his fleet of ships, which soon met disaster.

Sun Tzu advocated manipulating the enemy's agents to serve their own objectives.

This is a favorite game of both foreign investors who often deliberately discuss garbage over tapped telephones, and those Chinese counterparts who reveal false intentions through attractive translators wearing the latest imported outfits.

One foreign businessman who came to China with preconceived ideas about Chinese commercial espionage was convinced that the 1950s Soviet hotel he was staying in had a bug concealed somewhere in the architecture. He literally tore up his hotel room searching for the bug, which he was convinced must be hidden somewhere.

Finally, under the large Chinese carpet which dominated the room, he found a round metal plate with three screws fastening it to the floor. This must be the bug, he thought! He quickly took a coin out of his pocket and unscrewed the first screw. He then unscrewed the second screw. He was excited at the thought of finally discovering and exposing the bug planted in his room as he began to unscrew the third—only to have his anticipation rudely shattered when he heard the old Soviet-style chandelier in the room below crash to the floor.

Inflict Pain on Yourself in Order
to Infiltrate Your Adversary's Camp
and Win the Confidence of the Enemy

Interpretation: Absorb loss in order to win trust.
Inflict an injury on yourself to win confidence.

During the Spring and Autumn Period, the king of Zheng, in a strategy designed to erode the confidence of his enemy, the king of Hu, gave his favorite daughter to the king of Hu in marriage. In order to show his goodwill toward Hu, he then executed one of his own advisors who had advocated attacking Hu. Seeing all this, the king of Hu trusted that his border with the kingdom of Zheng would be safe from invasion. At that point, Zheng launched a surprise attack against Hu and conquered the Hu kingdom.

An assassin who attempted to kill the first Emperor, Qin Shi Huangdi, cut off the head of his best friend (who was on the Emperor's "wanted list") so as to gain an audience with the Emperor himself.

Foreign investors will often be impressed by the expense to which Chinese hosts will go to impress them with banquets, trips to local sightseeing places, and gifts. "Of course we trust our hosts ... they paid for everything," says the naive investor. Beware!

Many overseas Chinese returning to China come first as bearers of gifts before they ask for something in return. They will often donate some of the money they have earned overseas to building schools, roads and hospitals in the communities from which their parents or grandparents came.

While on the surface this may be seen as an act of goodwill and benevolence, it is, in reality, a clever strategic move. These overseas Chinese, by donating to the community from which their ancestors came, are not only fostering good relations with the officials who are in charge today, but creating a subtle kind of obligation, which these officials will have to repay by supporting any investment project which may come to the table at a future date. In this way, money spent as a loss on donations and gifts, is recouped later when one needs something done.

Lead Your Adversary to
Chain Together Their Warships

Interpretation: Turn your adversary's strength into
weakness. Lead your adversary on until he falls through
pride. It now also means: devise a set of interlocking
stratagems leading your adversary to defeat.

This strategy comes from the Three Kingdoms Period when
General Cao Cao was tricked into chaining his ships together
before ferrying troops across a turbulent river on the claim that
this would give the boats more stability. Cao Cao found to his
dismay that the enemy had intended for him to do this, so that
when they set fire to his ships, the ships would burn as one as
they were linked together with iron chains.

When doing business in China, don't "chain your ships
together." In addition, don't tie your own hands, or let your
company headquarters get you all tied up.

This mistake was made when one multinational sent a
Taiwanese manager to China to negotiate a deal based on the
assumption that because he spoke Mandarin he would have
some knowledge of how to deal with the Chinese in China.

Corporate headquarters was confident of its choice. Surprise!

The Taiwanese manager, concerned with covering his back, was aggressive from the beginning, and basically acted in the kind of pushy way that may be suitable for driving through Taipei rush hour traffic, but which is a recipe for disaster at a negotiation table in China.

The negotiations began with the Taiwanese making his first mistake of demanding all kinds of controls over the Chinese management. This was not a good idea, since it was the Chinese management who were negotiating with him. However, corporate headquarters favored this kind of tough approach, and insisted he maintain this line of attack.

The second mistake was to present the Chinese management with a contract so tightly worded that even if they were stupid, there would be no doubt that this joint venture was going to erode their power base. Corporate headquarters liked this kind of contract as it was drafted by American lawyers. They insisted that no changes be made at the negotiation table without clearance from the lawyers "back home."

The company's third mistake was when the representative showed up in China thinking that he would actually get the Chinese party to sign the contract and agree to the "castration" terms. All corporate eyes in headquarters were on the Taiwanese manager as they waited tensely for him to close the deal as quickly as possible—a deal which was supposed to be closed before the end of the year to fit neatly into that year's annual budget. The Christmas holidays were coming up. Everyone was waiting for the result. Hopes for the deal and decisions from the corporate side were inextricably linked.

"Clank" is the sound' of a wad of tobacco being spat into an aluminum spittoon. When the Taiwanese manager heard this sound, he should have realized it would be a long negotiation.

STRATEGY 36
Retreat is the Best Option

Interpretation: Opt out. Do not participate in or play the game that your adversary wants you to play.

During the Spring and Autumn Period, the king of Yue conquered the kingdom of Wu. Two men had stood by the king's side and contributed to his cause—Fan Li and Wen Zhong. Fan Li decided to withdraw from politics and go into business. Wen Zhong, however, remained faithful to the king of Yue. Later, however, the king of Yue had him killed because he was afraid that Wen Zhong might turn on him one day. The moral of the story is, "he who runs away today lives to do business another day."

As Mao Zedong said, "If the battle can be won, fight it; if not, depart." As one China trader reminisced, "When the Chinese want you to sign a contract in a hurry, they always tell you there is another party waiting on the sidelines who wants to do a deal with them, but 'because of their good relationship with you, they will give you first option'. When they told me this in Shanghai, and showed me the terms, all I could say was, if you have someone else who is actually willing to agree to these prices, as a 'friend' all I can say is you had better get them to sign up as quickly as possible. I certainly can't accept these terms and I don't know anyone else who would. They just went into silent shock."

One lawyer was locked in three weeks of negotiations in Beijing. His driver (who liked to drive him to meetings because he was often given cigarettes) was very frustrated because the lawyer spent three weeks locked in meetings and never came out. Finally, the driver left a message with the lawyer's secretary in his Beijing office: "Tell your clients that if they can't make money in China, then just go home!"

Glossary

The following are useful terms which you may encounter in your negotiations in China and in the text of this book.

Baole

A feeling, literally translated as "I'm stuffed," which is uttered at various stages of discomfort during a banquet when one is consuming a "menagerie" of foods—duck, snake, pigeon, turtle, abalone, and just about anything else which one might remember as a child from a visit to the zoo.

Bonding

A popular MBA yuppie buzz word which in China means sitting around the karaoke bar until 2:00 a.m. *ganbei*-ing one glass of XO after another with one's Chinese counterparts.

Cao Cao

A hero of the Three Kingdoms Period. "When you least expect him, he is there."

Courtesan

A maid in waiting at the Emperor's court during either the Three Kingdoms or Warring States Period. Someone who wears lots of make-up and is equipped with beeper and handphone. A person who knocks at your hotel room door at 2:30 a.m. when you have just returned from a successful bonding session and are about to begin the post-bonding syndrome.

Friendly Negotiation

A state of euphoria which is often not as friendly as one would like to believe.

Ganbei

An action best defined as "bottoms up." To be performed after a long and complimentary toast, and to be followed by showing one's guests the empty glass as proof that all the liqour has been drunk and as an expression of one's friendship and tolerance.

Get Me a Ticket to Hong Kong

A statement which one should remember how to say in Chinese.

Maotai

A fiery white rice wine which is kept in stone bottles because it eats through glass. A favorite liquor used for toasts at Chinese banquets.

Mutual Understanding

A feeling of disbelief if it can be believed. Something like Nirvana, which is rarely attained.

Post-bonding Syndrome

Vomiting all the XO and exotic food over one's bed in the hotel room at 3:00 a.m. after a successful bonding session.

Strategic Planning

For Western negotiators, this involves complex co-ordination between various corporate departments and the analysis of findings from various in-depth studies of the China market carried out by top-line international consulting groups, culminating in pre-negotiation strategic briefing sessions and post-negotiation strategic debriefing sessions. For Chinese negotiators, this means applying any of the 36 strategies set out in Part III of this book!

Sun Tzu

Literally translated as "Master Sun," the guru of strategy. A Chinese military master and philosopher who lived 2,000 years ago. The most popular name to use on the title of an MBA textbook.

Three Kingdoms

A novel which is actually more a history of three kingdoms (Wei, Wu and Shu) which fought against each other a little less than 2,000 years ago, and which has become the basis for many strategies contained in this book.

Warring States

A period of Chinese history when everyone fought against everyone else. Not to be confused with your joint venture's board of directors' meeting.

XO

A semi-sweet cognac which is supposed to be "extra old," thereby being dubbed "XO." A favorite liquor used for toasts in karaoke bars. A necessary purchase at the Duty Free shop before entering China on a negotiation trip.

Annex I

Chronology of Chinese Dynasties

Xia (21st–16th centuries BC)
The legendary first dynasty of China. It is unclear what happened then, but people believe that the I-Ching was developed during this period.

Shang (16th–11th centuries BC)
A prosperous period, famous for bronzes and pottery.

Western Zhou (11th century–770 BC)
Chinese culture began its ascent during this period. Written records remain intact. Law, education and ethics develop to new heights.

Eastern Zhou (770–256 BC)
Replaces Western Zhou and written records. Education and ethics move from western China to eastern China. Eventually, the whole thing collapses and the Spring and Autumn Period begins.

Spring and Autumn Period (722–481 BC)

Not to be confused with the Spring or Autumn Festivals in China.

Warring States Period (403–221 BC)

China was divided into many small kingdoms which fought against each other. Most of the stories contained in this book come from this period.

Qin (221–206 BC)

The first Emperor of China unified the country by defeating all of the states fighting among each other during the Warring States Period. He did so by adopting many of the strategies mentioned in this book. He built the Great Wall to prevent people outside China from adopting these strategies and using them against him. He was buried among a complete pottery replication of his army, known as the "Terracotta Warriors," which is a statement of his prowess and successful utilization of the strategies contained in this book, and is a famous tourist site in China today (responsible for bringing a great amount of foreign exchange into the country).

Western Han (206 BC–AD 9)

After the first Emperor died, nobody could step into his shoes, and other people adopted the strategies contained in this book and dropped the status quo. A new dynasty emerged called the Western Han. The story of Liu Bang, the first Emperor of this dynasty, is contained in this book.

Xin (AD 9–23)

A period of economic growth and stability in China. In the absence of fighting, most of the strategies contained in this book were not used and were saved for the Eastern Han Dynasty which followed.

Eastern Han (AD 25–220)

The calm of the Xin erupted in the chaos of the Eastern Han. Strategy 31 came from this period. The chaos eventually got out of hand and China was divided into three kingdoms.

Three Kingdoms (Wei, Shu, Wu) (AD 220–265)

This was a period when China split into three kingdoms which warred against each other and became the basis of China's epic, the *Romance of the Three Kingdoms*. Most of the strategies contained in this book which do not come from the Warring States Period come from the Three Kingdoms Period. The *Romance of the Three Kingdoms* became a classic text of strategy. Aside from Sun Tzu's *Art of War*, Mao Zedong adopted many of his own strategies from this epic.

Western Jin (AD 265–316)

This was a period of economic retraction and consolidation of assets by the power élite. People did not like it, however, and the Western Jin were replaced by the Eastern Jin.

Eastern Jin (AD 317–420)

This was a period of great military might because a new power élite removed the former power élite of the Western Jin (see above) using some of the strategies contained in this book.

Northern and Southern Dynasties (Song, Qi, Liang, Chen, Northern Wei, Eastern Wei, Western Wei, Northern Zhou) (AD 386–581)

China was divided into many different kingdoms which fought

against each other. Some of the strategies in this book were used during this period. Others were invented during this time. It was during this period that the compass was invented in China.

Shui (AD 581–618)
The Great Canal was dug during this dynasty. It is still being used today. In fact, some think it is more efficient than flying local planes in China, and safer as well.

Tang (AD 611–907)
One of China's most glorious dynasties. Great cultural heights were attained. Famous pottery horses were made, replicas of which can be purchased in most Friendship Stores in China. Great poetry was written, second only to that of the Song (see below).

Five Dynasties (Later Liang, Later Tang, Later Jin, Later Ban, Later Zhou) (AD 907–960)
As soon as one Emperor consolidated power, another removed him (using the strategies in this book).

Northern Song (AD 960–1127)
Before the Song were pushed south, they were known as the Northern Song.

Southern Song (AD 1127–1279)
Famous for their poetry, the Song were too busy with prose to do anything about the growing Mongol threat on their northern border. The result was that they were conquered.

Yuan (AD 1279–1368)

When Ghengis Khan conquered Europe, his grandson, Kublai, decided he needed something more challenging. The result was that the Mongols attacked the Southern Song in China, and took over the middle kingdom. During this period, Marco Polo visited China, bought gunpowder, and civilized Europe.

Ming (AD 1368–1644)

Famous for pottery (blue and white), the Ming reached one of the highest levels of cultural sophistication in China. Although simple in style, Ming-period furniture makes a great buy for any antique collector who has a chance to obtain a genuine piece.

Qing (AD 1644–1911)

The last dynasty and last emperor. Antiques from this period can be legally exported from China.

Annex II

Foreign Investors' Guide to Maotai Avoidance

In consideration of some of the trials and tribulations which foreign investors confront as part of their China business activities, some special, never before revealed, strategies of how to avoid excess Maotai intake during banquets associated with contract negotiations in China are given here:

(1) Doctor's Orders

One foreign investor regularly had his doctor issue him with a letter explaining that he was unable for medical reasons to drink Maotai or any other rice or grain liquor. Prior to each banquet, he met with the Chinese hosts in advance, showed them the letter and apologized, saying that although he would like to drink with them, he was under doctor's orders and would have to refrain. The Chinese inevitably understood and he was able to get away with intaking vast amounts of Coca Cola and mango juice instead.

(2) Bring along a Guest

A favorite practice of one investor was to bring a nightclub hostess with him to banquets as his "secretary." The woman's capacity for alcohol was amazing, and she was able to drink along with the comrades while he did the talking. The older officials were always titillated. The strategy appears to have worked successfully over a long period of time.

(3) Switch to Water

One negotiator always kept his assistant next to him, who was in charge of a bottle of mineral water under the table. While toasts were being made, the assistant would dump his own Maotai on the floor, fill the cup with mineral water and switch cups with his boss. This lasted through a number of successful banquets until somebody on the Chinese side suggested that as an expression of mutual bonding, they switch cups, drinking out of each other's cup. To the chagrin of the Chinese, it was discovered that the investor had been drinking water all along.

(4) Dump the Maotai on the Floor

Many negotiators, when the going gets exciting, and everyone is tossing Maotai down their throats, will suddenly find various techniques for tossing it onto the floor.

(5) Toss It over Your Shoulder

Other negotiators have developed the successful technique of tossing Maotai over their shoulders when everybody is tossing it down their throats with heads back. This worked successfully for one negotiator for a long period of time until at one banquet he found that every time he was tossing the Maotai over his shoulder it was hitting the back of the dress of an official's wife sitting at the table behind.

(6) Pour It in Your Lap

When one gets caught throwing Maotai on the floor or over his shoulder, he can instead discreetly pour it into his lap between alternate rounds of Maotai intake, pretending that he had an accident, excusing himself, going to the restroom, and spitting out the rest.

(7) Be Bold Now, Vomit Later

Some investors are willing to consume Maotai throughout a banquet, returning to their rooms later only to vomit everything before starting negotiations the next day. If one is particularly anxious to get the Maotai out of one's system, one can always stick a spoon down the back of one's throat. Alternatively, if one is patient, Maotai inevitably seeks its own level.

(8) Bring Schnapps

One businessman regularly brought German Schnapps to banquets. When the Maotai began flowing, he would start pouring rounds for his Chinese counterparts. For some biological reason, they could never stand Schnapps. So whenever the Maotai began to flow too much, he would bring out the Schnapps and force it upon his counterparts. It always had the effect of neutralizing the evening's excitement and slowing down the liquor intake.

(9) Outdrink the Others

One businessman had such a tolerance for alcohol, it is said that he was always able to outdrink the others. The story, as told, was that one day he was attending a banquet held at the Great Hall of the People, hosted by a branch of the PLA. He *ganbei*-ed so many Maotais that the General hosting the banquet finally called it quits as everyone else was getting sick. The businessman, however, was relentless and kept pressing the General to drink more with him. Holding the Maotai bottle and an empty cup, he encouraged the General with *lai lai* ("another round"), eventually backing the General out the doors of the Great Hall and into Tiananmen Square. As the story goes, he chased the General around Tiananmen Square with the Maotai bottle until some of the other officers intervened and explained to the businessman that "enough is really enough!"